365

DALAI LAMA

Also by His Holiness the Dalai Lama

A Simple Path
The Art of Living
The Dalai Lama's Book of Love and Compassion
The Dalai Lama's Book of Transformation
The Dalai Lama's Book of Wisdom
The Four Noble Truths
The Heart of the Buddha's Path
The Joy of Living and Dying in Peace
The Power of Compassion
The Way to Freedom
Transforming the Mind

365

DALAI LAMA

DAILY ADVICE FROM THE HEART

HIS HOLINESS THE
DALAI LAMA

Edited by Matthieu Ricard
Translated from the Tibetan by Christian Bruyat
(English translation by Dominique Messent)

HarperCollins *Publishers* India

HarperCollins *Publishers* India
by arrangement with
HarperCollins *Publishers* Limited

First published in 2001 as *conseils du Caeue*
by Presses de la Renaissance

Seventh impression 2026

Published in 2003 by Element,
an imprint of HarperCollins *Publishers*

ISBN 978-81-7223582-6

BUDDHISM

HarperCollins *Publishers*
A-75, Sector 57, NOIDA, Uttar Pradesh – 201301, India
1 London Bridge Street, London, SE1 9GF, United Kingdom
Hazelton Lanes, 55 Avenue Road, Suite 2900, Toronto, Ontario M5R 3L2
and 1995 Markham Road, Scarborough, Ontario M1B 5M8, Canada
25 Ryde Road, Pymble, Sydney, NSW 2073, Australia
195 Broadway, New York, NY 10007, USA

Printed and bound in India by
Manipal Technologies Limited

MIX
Paper | Supporting
responsible forestry
FSC™ C043100
FSC
www.fsc.org

This book is produced from independently certified FSC® paper
to ensure responsible forest management.

Contents

Acknowledgements

I personally wish to thank all those who helped this book see the light of day: Matthieu Ricard who recorded the Dalai Lama's words; Christian Bruyat who participated in the Tibetan conversations and translated them into French; Kusho Lhakdor, the Dalai Lama's personal translator, who transcribed the interviews to ensure the translation was faithful and who, with the Dalai Lama's permission, made available to us some pieces of advice that the Dalai Lama had given previously on a number of topics in this book; Mrs Yutock and Wangpo Bashi of the Office of Tibet in Paris who, together with Sylvie Fénart, assisted with the arrangements necessary for the completion of the project.

THE PUBLISHER, PRESSES DE LA RENAISSANCE

Foreword

The Dalai Lama's residence dominates the vast Indian plains that stretch away from its windows as far as the eye can see. To the north, a few snow-capped peaks remind the visitor that Tibet only lies about one hundred kilometres away as the crow flies; so near, yet so far.

Everywhere there is a feeling of peace and calm. People say little and speak softly, as if aware of the pointlessness of unnecessary words. The silence is punctuated only by Kundun's kindly peals of laughter. Kundun, meaning 'Presence', is the name used by Tibetans to refer to the Dalai Lama, and it reflects their love and respect for him.

In fact, for several months each year the Dalai Lama has to respond to everyone's aspirations, continuing to pursue the Tibetan cause even when it is suffocated by the implacable stranglehold of the Chinese dictatorship and overlooked by democracies that are more concerned about new markets than they are about justice. As a tireless pilgrim of peace, he works at the very centre of a whirlwind of activity where the few moments of respite are measured in minutes. And yet, despite the almost unbearable pace of his schedule, Kundun always maintains the same serenity and openness. Whoever he meets, whether it be an old friend, a visitor or a passer-by, he is instantly and completely present, gazing into each one's face with that special expression of goodness, simplicity and tremendous humour.

His message is always the same and he repeats it untiringly to anyone who cares to listen:

'Every single being, even those who are hostile to us, is just as afraid of suffering as we are, and seeks happiness in the same way as we do. Every person has the same right as we do to be happy and not to suffer. So let's take care of others wholeheartedly, of both our friends and our enemies. This is the basis for true compassion.'

A few years ago, Alain Noel, the director of the French publishers Presses de la Renaissance, thought of asking the Dalai Lama to write a 'spiritual testament'. On reflection, as we hope with all our hearts that the Dalai Lama will live to well over a hundred, it seemed more auspicious to ask him to give some simple pieces of advice aimed at a broad cross-section of people with differing personalities, social backgrounds and professions. It so happens that when advice of this kind was given by great masters in Tibet, it would often be compiled into a book and called 'Advice from the Heart'. So the subtitle and shape of this book emerged quite naturally.

Since the time he had available for interview was limited, we proposed a list of subjects that he was able to discard or develop at will. He personally added a number of subject areas which we had not thought of and which are close to his heart, in particular the concerns of prisoners and homosexuals.

Sometimes serious and sometimes playful, sometimes firm and sometimes pensive, and regularly punctuating his remarks with bursts of laughter, he really gave us the impression that he was talking freely without trying to please. He was intimately concerned by every human problem and yet, at the same time, he considered them dispassionately.

The Dalai Lama is known for his straight talking and the total absence of any desire to prove anything at all about himself or Buddhism. He often says, 'I am just a monk'. His only goal is to share his experience with others so he can help them to be happy in the most effective way possible.

He does not use fancy expressions or obscure terminology to mask any embarrassment or hesitation. If a problem does not have a clear solution in his mind, or if it does not correspond to a truth that he senses deeply, rather than avoiding it with a clever turn of phrase or a stereotyped answer, he states quite clearly that he is puzzled and does not hesitate to come out with a terse 'I don't know' that takes one by surprise and makes one smile.

For those who know him a little, there is no doubt that his

answers and the way he gives them reflect who he is and what he thinks. He never tries to appear otherwise.

His advice is often quite simple because he sees no point in being complicated. Some people may find it rather naïve to keep repeating *ad nauseam* that we must have 'good heart', and yet his insistence on this point does echo a reality: on the one hand, it is difficult truly to have a good heart, and on the other hand, if we don't cultivate this fundamental virtue within ourselves, any talk of world peace and other grand ideas is nothing more than idle prattle.

The Dalai Lama exhorts us to develop the potential for kindness and love that he believes we all possess. By appealing to our everyday experience, he shows us how to become 'a good human being' and make the most of our life. He continually emphasizes 'universal responsibility', the awareness that each one of us, as a member of the human family, can become a builder of peace and protector of beings. 'Outer disarmament depends on inner disarmament', he says frequently.

The simplicity of his words helps to direct us towards the main point. We should not take it for an inability to express profound or complex ideas. Whenever the subject of a teaching or an interview touches upon difficult issues in philosophy, metaphysics or spirituality, the Dalai Lama displays such a rich understanding of different views that the depth of his comments often disarms the best of scholars.

This is how His Holiness the Dalai Lama offered us his 'advice from the heart'. He spoke in Tibetan, and the recordings were translated by Christian Bruyat and myself. The atmosphere was relaxed, intimate and joyful. He wanted to say things that could help everyone in developing a 'secular spirituality', so wherever the topic allowed, he took care to avoid specifically Buddhist concepts. There is no doubt that if we could truly assimilate into our thoughts and actions just a fraction of his advice, we would only rejoice at the results.

MATTHIEU RICARD,
SHECHEN MONASTERY, NEPAL,
16 JUNE 2001

INTRODUCTION:
MEDITATIONS ON LIVING

Common sense shows that human life is short-lived and that it is best to make of our brief sojourn on this Earth something that is useful to oneself and others.

2

As humans, we all have the same potential, unless there is some sort of retarded brain function. The wonderful human brain is the source of our strength and the source of our future, provided we utilize it in the right direction. If we use the brilliant human mind in the wrong way, it really is a disaster.

3

I think human beings are the superior sentient beings on this planet. Humans have the potential not only to create happy lives for themselves, but also to help other beings. We have a natural creative ability and it is very important to realize this.

We cannot be useful to ourselves unless we are also useful to others. Whether we like it or not, we are all connected, and it is unthinkable to be happy all by oneself. Anyone who is only concerned by his own well-being will suffer eventually. Anyone who is only concerned with the well-being of others takes care of himself without even thinking about it. Even if we decide to remain selfish, let us be intelligently selfish – let us help others!

5

We do not usually know how to distinguish between what is essential and what is secondary. We spend our lives running about here and there after pleasures that are forever eluding us and leaving us unsatisfied. We try to be happy come what may, without wondering whether we are causing anyone else to suffer in the process. We are prepared to do anything to amass and defend our possessions, which are neither lasting nor true sources of happiness.

6

*O*ur mind is full of anger, jealousy, and other negative feelings, and we do not realize that such feelings are incompatible with inner peace and joy. Our intelligence, which is the glory of human beings, is used only to deceive others and to gain more for ourselves at others' expense. At the end of the day we find only suffering and, as the ultimate absurdity, we lay the blame for this on other people.

7

Let's use our human intelligence wisely. Otherwise, how are we superior to animals?

8

*I*f we really want to make our lives meaningful and happy, we should begin by thinking sanely. We should cultivate the human qualities we all possess but which we bury under a heap of confused thinking and conflicting emotions.

9

Let us cultivate love and compassion, both of which give true meaning to life. This is the religion I preach, more so than Buddhism itself. It is simple. Its temple is the heart. Its teaching is love and compassion. Its moral values are loving and respecting others, whoever they may be. Whether one is a layperson or a monastic, we have no other option if we wish to survive in this world.

10

To be kind, honest and have positive thoughts; to forgive those who harm us and treat everyone as a friend; to help those who are suffering and never to consider ourselves superior to anyone else: even if this advice seems rather simplistic, make the effort of seeing whether by following it you can find greater happiness.

11

We do not need to reflect too long before we realize that all beings spontaneously look for happiness and try to avoid suffering. You will not find even a single insect that will not do everything in its power to escape suffering and to feel good. Human beings have the additional capacity to think. So we should make good use of our intelligence.

12

Pleasure and suffering are based on sensory perceptions and inner satisfaction. For us, inner satisfaction is the more important of these. It is special to human beings. With a few exceptions, animals are not able to experience this.

13

Satisfaction is characterized by inner peace. It arises from generosity, honesty and what I call ethical conduct, that is, a way of behaving that respects the right of others to happiness.

14

A great deal of our suffering comes from having too many thoughts. And, at the same time, the way we think is not sane. We are only concerned by our immediate satisfaction and forget to measure its long-term advantages and disadvantages, either for ourselves or for others. But such an attitude always goes against us in the end. There is no doubt that by changing our way of seeing things we could reduce our current difficulties and avoid creating new ones.

15

There are certain types of suffering, such as the suffering associated with birth, sickness, old age and death that cannot be avoided. The only thing we can do is reduce the fear they instil in us. But there are many other problems in the world, from marital quarrels to the most devastating wars, that could be avoided if only we adopted a sane and healthy attitude.

16

If we do not think through things well, if our vision is only short-term and our methods only superficial, and if we do not consider things with an open and relaxed outlook, then we turn what started as minor problems into major difficulties. In other words, we ourselves create a great deal of our own suffering.

Meditations on Young People

17

Whether it be in our refugee schools or by chance in the course of visiting India or another country, I am always glad to meet young people. They are direct and sincere, and their minds are more open and flexible than those of adults. When I see a child, my first thought, from the bottom of my heart, is that he or she is my own child or a longstanding friend who I should care for with all my love.

18

The most important thing with children is to ensure that their education is complete in the broadest sense – not only gaining knowledge but also developing basic human qualities. The foundations of our lives are laid in childhood. The way of thinking that we learn during those critical years will have a profound effect on our lives, in the same way as food and physical hygiene will affect our future health.

19

*I*f young people do not put all their effort into study, it will be difficult for them to fill this gap later on. I have discovered this myself. Sometimes I would lose interest in what I was studying and not put so much effort into it. I have regretted that ever since. I always tell myself that I missed out on something at that time. On the basis of this experience, I always advise young people to consider their school years as one of the most important times of their life.

20

Right from childhood, one must also learn to get on with others and help them. Quarrels and minor conflicts are inevitable, but the main thing is to get used to wiping the slate clean and never harbouring grudges.

21

Sometimes we imagine that children do not think about serious things, such as death. But when I hear the questions they ask themselves, I realize that they often do think about serious matters, especially on what happens after death.

22

*I*t is in childhood that our intelligence blossoms and our minds overflow with questions. This intense desire for knowledge is the basis of personal growth. The more we are curious about the world and want to know how and why things are the way they are, the clearer our minds become and the more we develop a spirit of initiative.

23

*I*n modern society, we tend to overlook what I call natural human qualities – kindness, compassion, understanding, and forgiveness. In childhood it is easy to make friends. You only have to laugh with someone once and immediately you are friends. Children do not ask about each other's race or profession. The main thing is that the other person is a human being like us and that we relate to him or her.

24

As we grow up we attach less and less importance to affection, friendship, and mutual support. Instead, we emphasize race, religion, or nationality. We forget the main thing and concentrate on the most trivial.

25

I ask those of you who are 15 or 16 years old not to let go of that freshness you had in your childhood, and to value it always. Reflect over and over again on what makes us human inside, and build on this to gain unwavering trust in your own nature and find your self-confidence.

It is important to realize early on that life is not easy. In order to make the best of it and not to lose courage when problems arise, it is essential to acquire inner strength.

26

People attach a great deal of value to individualism and to each person's right to think for themselves without conforming to the values imposed by society or tradition. That is good. But on the other hand, people acquire information only from outside sources, through the media and, in particular, through television. These have become our only reference points and our only sources of inspiration. This extreme dependence makes us incapable of holding our own or of using our own personal qualities, and as a result we lack confidence in our true nature.

27

*I*t seems to me that self-confidence and the ability to stand one's ground are essential if we want to succeed in life. I am not talking of stupid self-assurance but of an awareness of our inner potential, a certainty that we can always correct our behaviour, improve ourselves, enrich ourselves, and that things are never hopeless.

28

The favourite subjects in the media tend to be robberies, crimes, and actions motivated by avarice or hatred. And yet it is not true to say that nothing noble happens in the world, that nothing arises from our good human qualities. Aren't there people who look after the sick, orphans, the elderly, and the handicapped, without any desire to make money? Aren't there people who act out of love for others? In fact, there are many such people, but we have become used to thinking that this type of negative behaviour is normal.

29

I am convinced that naturally, deep inside, we do not like to kill, rape, rob, lie or commit other negative actions, and that each one of us is capable of love and compassion. Let's remember what a critical role affection plays in our lives, from birth onwards. Without affection, we would have been dead long ago. Think of how good we feel when we are surrounded by the love of other people and when we ourselves love others; and think of how, by contrast, uncomfortable we feel with ourselves when anger or hatred take us over.

30

Loving thoughts and actions are clearly beneficial for our physical and mental health. They express our true nature. On the contrary, violent, cruel, and hateful acts shock us. That is why we feel the need to talk about them and why they make front-page news. The problem is that little by little, insidiously, we come to think that human nature is wicked. One day we might convince ourselves that there is no hope for mankind.

31

I think it is essential to say to young people: recognize the human qualities that are naturally present within you. Build an unwavering confidence on their foundations and learn to stand on your own two feet!

32

Some young people start off in life without really knowing what they want. They take up a job, find they don't like it, leave it, start another, leave that, and end up dropping everything and thinking there is nothing that can inspire them.

If this applies to you, you should realize that life is never easy. Do not expect that everything will suddenly work for you and that all your problems will miraculously go away.

33

When you look for a job after your studies are finished, look for something that suits your personality, knowledge, skills and interests, and maybe even something that suits your family background. It may be sensible to learn a profession that others around you practise already. Then you can benefit from their advice and experience.

Take all factors into account, think of what opportunities are the most appropriate for your situation, and then make your choice. Once you have made your choice, stick with it. Even if you come across problems, have the determination to overcome them. Be confident, and put all your energy into it.

34

*I*f you think of the career opportunities on offer as so many dishes that you can taste one after the other, without eating any single one, then your chances of success are slim. You should realize that one day or another you will have to make a decision and that there is nothing in this world that does not have any disadvantages at all.

35

Sometimes I think that we behave like spoilt children. When we are very little, we depend entirely on our parents. Then we go to school, we are educated, we are fed, we are clothed, and the weight of our problems is still on the shoulders of other people. When the moment finally comes for us to take charge of our own life and to carry our own burden, we imagine that everything will go smoothly! Unfortunately, such an attitude defies reality. In this world, everyone without exception has problems.

Meditations on Adulthood

36

The job we do is our way of earning a living, but it is also the way we contribute to the society on which we depend. In fact, the relationship between ourselves and society is a reciprocal one. If society is prosperous then we will benefit, and if it is not we will suffer. Our community also influences other communities around it and ultimately the whole of humanity.

37

*I*f the inhabitants of your region are economically successful, that prosperity will benefit the whole country. The French economy, for example, is linked with that of Europe, and the European economy is linked to the rest of the world. Modern societies depend closely on each other and the behaviour of one affects all the others. Realizing this is of paramount importance.

38

When I say that the health of a society will have natural repercussions on each one of us, I do not mean to imply that it is necessary to sacrifice one's own well-being for that of the group. All I am saying is that the two are inseparable. Nowadays, we tend to think that the fate of society and that of the individual are two different things. It is the individual that matters, not the community. If we broaden our field of vision just a little, we will see that in the long-term this attitude does not make sense.

39

The happiness and suffering of human beings does not depend on satisfying the senses alone. Above all, they depend on mental factors. Let's not forget that. If you have a beautifully furnished house, a luxury car in your garage, money in the bank, good social status, and the recognition of your peers, it does not necessarily follow that you will be happy. Even if you become a billionaire, will it automatically make you happy? Maybe not.

40

The profound pleasure that we gain from looking at a painting or listening to music shows how important it is for human beings to have inner satisfaction rather than the gross pleasures of the senses or the possession of material goods.

Nevertheless, even aesthetic satisfaction depends largely on vision and hearing, so it can only yield temporary well-being and this is not so fundamentally different from the satisfaction produced by drugs. When we leave the museum or the concert hall, our aesthetic pleasure is over and is replaced by the desire to experience it again. It never brings true inner happiness.

41

*I*nner contentment is the main thing. Do not give up your basic needs; we all have the right to the basic minimum. We need it to live and we should make sure we have it. If that means protest, then let's protest. If we have to strike, then let's go on strike. But we should not fall into extreme attitudes. If we are never satisfied inside and are always looking for more, we won't be happy and will always feel there is something lacking.

42

*I*nner happiness is not determined by material circumstances or sensual gratification. It depends on our mind. The most vital thing is to recognize how important this kind of happiness really is.

Meditations on Growing Old

43

When we grow old, if we have no religious faith the most important thing to recognize is that our fundamental sufferings – birth, sickness, old age, and death – are an inherent part of life. As soon as we have taken birth, we cannot avoid growing old and dying. That is how it is. It is pointless to say this is unfair or that it should be different.

According to Buddhism, the opportunity of a long life is due to the merit we have gained in the past. Even if you are not a Buddhist, think of people who die young and be joyful that your life has been a long one.

45

*I*f the first part of your life was lived to the full, remember that at that time you contributed to society and your work was useful and carried out with sincere intentions. So now you have nothing to regret.

46

If you have a religious faith, then pray or meditate according to your religion. If your mind is still clear, reflect on the fact that birth, sickness, old age and death are part of every human life and are inescapable. Recognizing this and accepting it fully will help you to grow old more peacefully.

47

I will soon be 68 years old. If from time to time I did not accept deep down that my physical body has grown older over the years, I would find it difficult to come to terms with my condition. When you are old, be aware of what that really means, without deceiving yourself, and try to make the most of it.

48

Ask yourself what you can still contribute to the society on which you depend. With the knowledge you have gained, you can certainly be more useful to others than people who have not lived so long. Talk about your life with your family and your loved ones, and share your experiences with them. If you enjoy being with your grandchildren, communicate some of your understanding as you are looking after them and help to educate them.

Above all, do not end up like those old people who complain and quarrel all day long. Do not waste your energy in that way. Nobody will like you and old age will become a real tribulation.

MEDITATIONS ON MEN AND WOMEN

Men and women are, of course, physically different and this entails a number of differences on the emotional level. But their way of thinking, their sensations and every other aspect of their personalities are basically the same. Men are more able to do heavy work; women seem more efficient at tasks which require clear and quick thinking. Men and women are usually equals in areas where reflection plays a key role.

50

Since there are no fundamental differences between men and women, it goes without saying that they have the same rights and any discrimination is unjustified. In addition, men need women just as much as women need men.

Whenever their rights are trampled, women should demand their rights and men should support their struggle. I myself have fought in India for twenty years so that women can be educated, for example, and have jobs at every level of Tibetan society in an equal capacity to men.

51

According to Buddhism, there is not the slightest difference in the way both men and women have what we call Buddha nature, or the potential for enlightenment. They are therefore essentially equal.

52

*I*n certain traditions, men and women have always been segregated. But this was mostly for social and cultural reasons. Nagarjuna, in his *Precious Garland*, speaks of the 'defects of a woman's body'. Yet his intention was not to prove that women are inferior. It so happened that most monastics were men. The defects he mentioned were raised for the sole purpose of helping these men overcome their desire for women. Naturally, nuns should analyse men's bodies in a similar way.

53

*I*n the highest practices of Vajrayana, not only is there no segregation between men and women, but the feminine element plays such a vital role that contempt for women is considered a transgression of the vows.

Meditations on the Family

The family is the most fundamental unit in society. If it is ruled by peace and human values, then not only will parents live happily and free of tension, but their children and grandchildren will too, and even generations after that. If they have a religious faith, their children will naturally be drawn to this. If they speak politely to each other and behave ethically[1], love each other and have mutual respect, if they help those in need and show concern for the world around them, it is highly likely that their children will follow suit and become responsible people.

On the other hand, if the mother and father are continuously fighting and insulting each other, if they just do whatever comes into their heads without thinking of others, then not only will they never be happy themselves, but their children will inevitably fall victim to their influence.

1. To behave ethically, in the Buddhist sense that the Dalai Lama is referring to here, means to refrain from doing anything that might harm others.

55

As a Buddhist, I often tell Tibetans that if there is one area where they should make a real effort to re-establish and develop the Buddha's teaching, it is within their own families. That is where parents should express their faith, teach their children and truly become spiritual guides. They should not be content with simply showing their children pictures and explaining that they represent such and such a deity: they should fully explain that this deity symbolizes compassion, and that deity represents supreme wisdom, and so forth. The more parents understand the Buddhist teaching, the more they will be able to influence their children in a positive way. And this principle is of course valid for other spiritual or religious traditions too.

56

*O*ne family influences another, and then another, then ten, a hundred, and a thousand, and thus the whole of society will be better off.

57

When some people complain that nobody has any respect any more, whereas in less industralized countries people generally behave more responsibly, they should be careful to qualify such a statement.

The Indian regions in the Himalayas, for example, are quite inaccessible and are relatively free from the effects of modern technology. It is a fact that there are very few burglaries or murders there and that people are content with what they have. There are even some places where it is traditional to leave one's door open when one goes out, so that any visitors can make themselves at home and refresh themselves as they wait for their host to return. By contrast, in large cities like Delhi there is a lot of crime; people are never happy with their lot and this creates innumerable problems. But in my view, we are wrong to use this as a pretext for deciding that economic development is undesirable and that we should put the clock back.

58

The levels of understanding and respect found in traditional societies are often dictated by the survival conditions, and contentment also depends on temporary ignorance of other possible ways of life. Ask Tibetan nomads if they would prefer to be better protected from the winter cold, if they would like stoves that did not blacken the inside of their tents, if they would like to be better cared for when they are ill, or if they would be interested to see what is happening on the other side of the world by means of television. I know exactly what they would answer.

59

Economic and technological progress is desirable and necessary. It is the culmination of many factors so complex that they escape us and it would be naïve to think that we can solve all our problems simply by halting progress. However, it definitely should not take place haphazardly. It should go hand in hand with the development of moral values. It is our responsibility as human beings to ensure that these two tasks are accomplished simultaneously. This is the key to our future. A society in which material development co-exists with spiritual progress is one where true happiness is really possible.

60

*I*t is the family that must play the most important role. If peace truly reigns within the family, if the family imparts not only knowledge but true moral values, and is a place where one learns to live in an upright and altruistic way, then it becomes possible to build the rest of society on these foundations. For me, the family unit has an enormous responsibility.

61

*I*t is important that children are able to flourish within the family in the truest sense, that they develop their basic human qualities in its fold, that their behaviour is noble, they have the strength of mind to help others, feel concerned about their environment and serve as an example to others. Later on, such children will be good at their work and capable of training the next generation. Even if they become aged professors with thick spectacles, they will still retain some of the good habits they developed in their childhood. That is what I believe.

62

*I*f a family is to be successful, the man and woman must not come together simply because they are attached to each other's physical appearance, to the sound of the other's voice or other external features. They should begin by getting to know each other well. If each one discovers that the other has certain qualities and love becomes mutual, such love will naturally be associated with respect and consideration, and it is then highly likely that their marriage will be happy and long lasting.

63

If a man and woman marry through mere desire and sexual attraction, rather like the attraction one might have to a prostitute, without knowing the other person's character or holding them with respect, they will love each other only as long as their desire remains strong. But once the novelty of excitement has faded, if love does not go hand in hand with deep and mutual admiration, it becomes difficult to live together in harmony. This type of love is blind. After a while it often turns into its opposite. If the couple have children, then the children, too, run the risk of being unloved. It is very important to reflect on these things when one wishes to live with someone.

64

*O*ne day, I met a Christian priest in San Francisco who was counselling young people about marriage. He would tell them all that they should first get to know many boys or girls, and make their choice only after that. If they relied on a single encounter, they ran the risk of deceiving themselves. I found this approach very sound.

65

From the moment you get married, there are two of you. Even when we are alone, the thoughts we have in the evening might be the opposite of the thoughts we had in the morning. Needless to say, when two people are involved, differences of opinion can crop up at any time. If one partner or another is only interested in his or her own ideas and does not take the other's views into account, the couple is dysfunctional.

66

As soon as we live with another person, we should treat that person affectionately and always pay attention to how they think and feel. Each partner should carry his or her share of responsibility, whatever happens. Marriage cannot be the responsibility of just one partner.

67

The man should satisfy the woman, and the woman should satisfy the man. If neither does what the other wishes, the only possible outcome is conflict and separation. As long as no children are involved, this is not a disaster. One goes to court, fills in a few forms and all one does is waste paper. But if there are children, they will feel a deep sense of unease for the rest of their lives.

68

Many couples break up these days. Sometimes they have good reason for doing so, but in my view it would be better if before splitting up, they each did their utmost in order to live together happily. Of course, that requires personal effort and reflection. If separation is inevitable, the main thing is that it should happen as smoothly as possible without harming anyone.

69

*I*f you decide to live with someone, take the situation to heart and do not rush into it. Once you are together, reflect on the responsibilities of married life. Raising a family is a serious business. Do everything in your power to make it a happy family, to meet everyone's needs, to educate your children and ensure their future happiness.

70

Always choose quality over quantity. This rule applies to every life situation. In a monastery, it is better to have fewer monks but monks who are genuine. In a school, the main thing is not to have a large number of pupils but to educate them well. In a family, the best thing is not to have a large number of children but to have children who are healthy and well brought up.

Meditations on Being Single

There are many different ways of being unmarried. There are monastics who have taken the vow of chastity and laypeople who do not have a partner; there are those who are unmarried by choice and those who are unmarried despite themselves; there are those who are happily unmarried and those who find it very hard.

72

Married life offers some advantages but also produces its share of problems. One must devote a lot of time to one's partner and to one's children – if one has any; one has to spend time with them, accept there are great expenses, work harder, develop relations with the in-laws, and so on.

73

People who live alone generally lead a simpler life. There is only one stomach to fill, they have fewer responsibilities and are free to do what they want. If they are looking for a spiritual path or if they follow one already, they are free to go wherever their quest takes them. All they need is a suitcase and they can stay where they like for as long as they need. Celibacy can be a useful option in the sense that it allows us more freedom and efficiency to devote ourselves to whatever we wish to do.

74

Some men are alone despite their desperate attempts at finding a woman. Certain women are dying to meet the man of their life but never manage to fulfil their dream. Sometimes their problem stems from the fact they are too self-centred and too demanding of others. If they gradually adopt the reverse attitude and begin opening up to others whilst paying less attention to their own problems, they will elicit a naturally positive response from other people.

Meditations on Community Life

75

When community life is based on voluntary work, I think it is a very good thing. It is justified because people depend naturally on each other. Living in a community is rather like living in an enormous family that meets our needs.

76

We join a group because we find it has certain qualities. We enjoy working with others. Each person undertakes his or her daily tasks and receives a share of the common effort. It seems a practical solution to me.

77

*I*n every group different points of view will occur. But I see this as an advantage. The more we come across different opinions, the greater our opportunity to gain a greater understanding of others and to improve ourselves. If we battle against anyone who thinks differently from us, everything becomes hard. We should not hold rigidly to our personal views but enter into dialogue in an open-minded way.
In this way we will be able to compare viewpoints and discover new ones.

78

Whether it be within families or within other social groups, it is always important to engage in dialogue. From childhood, whenever there is a quarrel we should avoid having negative thoughts and thinking, 'How can I get rid of this person?' Without going as far as lending them a hand, at least let us try to listen to what they to say. We should train ourselves in this way. Whenever a quarrel breaks out at school or at home, we should immediately try to talk, and learn from the exchange.

79

We tend to think that if we disagree with someone, this automatically means there will be conflict, and that conflicts end with a winner and a loser or with wounded pride, as the expression goes. Let us avoid seeing things in this light. Let us always look for common ground. The key is to show immediate interest in the other's point of view. Surely this is something we can manage.

MEDITATIONS ON LIVING A LIFE OF PLENTY

80

When I meet people who are wealthy, I usually tell them that according to Buddhist teaching, wealth is a good sign. It is the fruit of a certain merit and the proof that they have been generous in the past. However, wealth is not synonymous with happiness. If it were, the richer one was the happier one would be.

81

As individuals, there is nothing fundamentally different about people who are wealthy. Even if they have an immense fortune, they cannot eat more than others since they have only one stomach; and they do not have extra fingers on their hands on which to wear rings. Of course, they can drink the most refined and expensive wines and spirits, and eat the most delicious foods. Unfortunately, these often harm their health. Many of those who are not obliged to work physically spend a lot of their energy keeping fit for fear of getting fat or falling ill. They are just like me; I do not often go out for a walk, and each day I have to use the bicycle in my room! When you think about it, it is not worth being rich if that is where it gets you!

82

There is, of course, the exhilarating feeling of being able to say to oneself, 'I am rich!' It brings a certain energy and can project an interesting social image. But does this really warrant all the stress associated with acquiring and increasing one's fortune? A rich person often offends part of the family or society in the process, and makes other people jealous and malicious. As a result, one is continually anxious and on the defensive.

83

*I*t seems to me that the only advantage of being rich is being able to help others. Socially, one plays a more important role and has greater influence. If one has good intentions one can do a great deal of good. If, on the other hand, one is malevolent, one can do more harm.

I often say that we are responsible for this Earth. So if we are able, thanks to our wealth, to do something useful and yet do not act, we are mindless idiots.

84

Every day we use food and goods that others produce for us. As soon as we have enough to live, we should help the rest of the world. How sad it would be to live a life of luxury without contributing to the happiness of those who are less fortunate than ourselves.

85

There are some extremely poor people. Some do not have basic food and shelter, not to mention education or health care. If we are rich and only look after ourselves, what are these people going to think? How should people react when they work hard from dawn to dusk earning next to nothing, and see others in the lap of luxury without appearing to lift a finger? Aren't we giving them reason to feel jealous and bitter? Are we not nudging them towards hatred and violence?

86

*I*f you have a lot of money, the best way of using it is to help the poor and those who are suffering, and generally to make the inhabitants of this Earth a little happier by providing solutions to their problems. Helping the poor does not only mean giving them money. It means above all providing education and health care, and helping people to be self-sufficient.

87

*I*t is pointless to live in luxury for oneself alone. Rather than spend your life wasting your money in useless luxuries, use it to benefit others. If you take pleasure from showing off your fortune or spending large sums on gambling, there is nothing much one can say as long as you are not harming anyone, because your money is your own. Nevertheless, you are deceiving yourself and squandering your life.

88

*I*f you are rich, you should also be aware that you are a human being, and in this respect you are no different from the poor man: you need the richness of inner happiness, and that happiness cannot be bought.

89

At the moment, the gap between rich and poor is getting wider. Over the last 20 years, there have been at least 500 new dollar billionaires. In 1982 there were only 12. Amongst these, over 100 are Asian nationals. Generally, one thinks of Asia as poor and yet there are countless poor people in Europe and America. The question of wealth and poverty therefore goes beyond a straightforward opposition between East and West.

90

Great ideologies like communism have totally failed in their attempts to force the rich to share their possessions. Now, people themselves have to realize the need to share. That naturally requires a profound change in attitudes and a new education.

91

*I*n the long run, the wealthy have nothing to gain in allowing the global situation to deteriorate. They will have to protect themselves from the resentment of the poor and will live in fear more and more, as is already the case in a number of countries. Any society where the rich are too rich and the poor too poor will generate violence, crime and civil war. Agitators can easily get the poor to rise up by making them think they are fighting for their cause. Many kinds of problems will ensue.

92

*I*f you are wealthy and help the poor around you, and if thanks to your efforts they enjoy better health and have the opportunity to develop their skills and knowledge, they will appreciate you in return. Even if you are rich, you will be their friend. They will be satisfied and so will you, don't you think? If misfortune befalls you, they will sympathise. But if, on the other hand, you close yourself up in your selfishness and do not share anything, they will hate you and will be pleased when you suffer. We are all social beings. When our environment is friendly, we automatically have trust and feel happier.

MEDITATIONS ON LIVING IN POVERTY

93

Material poverty should not prevent you from having noble thoughts. And in fact, these are far more important than wealth. That is why, as long as one has a human brain and body, even if one is poor, one has the main thing, so there is no reason to feel discouraged or to retreat inside oneself.

༩༤

*I*n India, I say to the lower caste people who are fighting for their rights that we are all human beings, we have the same potential, and that they should not be discouraged if they are poor and rejected by the other castes.

95

*I*t is useless to be bitter and to revolt against those who have possessions. Of course, the rich should respect the poor and if they abuse their power the poor should defend themselves. But cultivating envy and jealousy does not lead anywhere. If you want to be rich yourself, it is better to make the effort to have a good education rather than to sit back and complain. The main thing is to have the means to stand on one's own two feet.

96

I always think of the thousands of Tibetans who took refuge in India after my exile. They had lost everything, even their country, and most had no money, no shelter and no health care. They had to rebuild their life from nothing in very difficult circumstances, with only tents to protect them from the heat and the monsoons. They had to clear the patches of jungle that were allocated to them, and they died in their hundreds of diseases that were unknown in Tibet. And yet very few lost hope, and with surprising speed they succeeded in overcoming these difficulties and rediscovering the joy of life. This shows that with the right attitude, one can be happy even in the worst situations. But, on the other hand, if we have no inner peace, we deceive ourselves into thinking that comfort and prosperity will bring happiness.

97

Each one of us is free to complement material poverty with inner poverty. But it is preferable to cultivate a positive attitude. Here again, that does not mean that one should no longer make an effort not to be poor. If you are the victim of injustice, fight for your rights and ensure that the truth is victorious; that is important. In democratic societies, it is a great advantage that everyone is subject to the law. But always keep a just and kindly attitude.

Meditations on Sickness

98

These days, there are many medical advances. But our attitude of mind continues to play a crucial role in both prevention and cure. This is quite clear.

The body and mind are closely connected, and each influences the other. That is why you should never lose hope, however seriously sick you may be. Tell yourself that there is always a remedy and that you have a chance of recovering.

99

Whatever your situation, remember that worrying is pointless; it only adds to the suffering you already have. I often cite a very useful expression by the Indian sage Shantideva, who basically said this: If there is a solution, what is the point in being anxious? Be content to apply it. And if there is no solution, what is the point in being anxious? Anxiety will only make your suffering worse.

100

The best medicine is prevention. This is linked to diet and habitual behaviour. Many people abuse alcohol and tobacco. For a slight and fleeting pleasure from the taste and the power of these substances, they ruin their health. Others make themselves ill by overeating. I know Buddhist practitioners who do retreats and remain in good health as long as they stay in the mountain hermitage. But as soon as they go down and visit their families or friends, for New Year or other festivals, they can no longer control their appetite and fall sick. [Laughs.]

101

The Buddha used to say to his monks that if they didn't eat enough they would weaken their bodies and this is a mistake; but he would also tell them that by living a life that was too comfortable they would exhaust their merit. In this way, he was exhorting us to reduce our desires, to be satisfied with what we have and develop spiritually, but at the same time to keep healthy. Whether one eats too much or too little, in either case one will eventually fall ill. We should avoid any extremes in our daily life.

MEDITATIONS ON THE DISABLED AND THEIR CARERS

102

If you are physically disabled, you should tell yourself that deep down we are all the same. Even if you cannot use certain senses, your mind works in the same way as others' minds. Do not be discouraged, find confidence in yourself. You are a human being and you can make something of your life.

One day I visited a school for the dumb. At first sight, the children were unable to communicate in the way we usually do. But, in fact, they simply used other means and they were able to study just like anyone else. These days, even the blind can read and write with the help of machines. Some are even writers. On Indian television, I once saw a man who wrote with his feet. He did not write very quickly but he was able to form his letters very well.

103

Whatever happens, never lose heart. Whoever says to himself, 'I will succeed' will reach his goal. But if you think 'It's impossible, I don't have all my faculties, I will never manage', then you will fail. As the Tibetan saying goes, 'One cannot shake off poverty by losing courage.'

104

When a child is born disabled, it goes without saying that his or her father, mother, and other relatives, will go through moments of sadness, anxiety and despair. And yet, from another point of view, caring for others is a source of happiness and satisfaction. One reads in Buddhist texts that we should have more love for those who are suffering and cannot defend themselves. The more we help them, the more we can feel the profound satisfaction that comes from feeling useful.

105

As a general rule, caring for others is the best thing we can do. If it so happens that in your own home or nearby, there is someone who is completely vulnerable, defenceless and prisoner of an incurable disability, then reflect on the unique opportunity this provides you and serve that person joyfully. That is an excellent thing to do.

On the other hand, if you take it as an obligation and a nuisance, your activity will be incomplete, and you will create difficulties unnecessarily.

Meditations on the Dying and Their Carers

106

Death is a critical time, so it is very helpful to prepare oneself for it. We should reflect on the fact it is unavoidable. We should acknowledge that it is an integral part of life, since life necessarily has a beginning and an end. It is futile to try to escape it.

If such thoughts are rooted in our mind from an early age, when death comes it will not seem like the sudden occurrence of an abnormal event. We will be able to face it quite differently.

107

*I*t is true to say that most of us dislike thinking about our own death. We spend most of our lives amassing possessions or embarking on an endless number of projects, as though we were going to live for ever, as though it was not absolutely certain that one day – tomorrow perhaps, or even in the next moment – we will leave everything behind.

108

According to Buddhism, it is important to train ourselves right now so that we can die well. When our vital functions cease, the gross level of consciousness dissolves and the subtle consciousness, which does not depend on a physical support, manifests and offers a unique opportunity to the seasoned practitioner to progress towards enlightenment. That is why, particularly in the Tantras, one finds many meditation methods aimed at preparing the practitioner for the moment of death.

109

*I*f you are a religious person, then at the moment of death you should reconnect with your faith and pray. If you believe in God, tell yourself that even if it is sad to come to the end of one's life, God must have his reasons and death is something profound that you are unable to fathom. This thought will definitely help you.

110

*I*f you are a Buddhist and believe in rebirth, then death is just a change of physical body, rather like the way one swaps old clothes for new ones once they are worn out. When our physical support is no longer capable of keeping us alive due to internal and external causes, the time has come to give it up and take a new one. In these conditions, dying does not mean that we cease to exist.

111

When talking about the nature of impermanence we must bear in mind that there are two levels. One is the coarse level, which is quite obvious and is the cessation of a life or an event. But the impermanent nature which is being taught in the Four Noble Truths refers to the more subtle aspect of impermanence, which is the transitory nature of existence.

112

By reflecting on the coarser levels of impermanence, one will be able to confront and counteract grasping at permanence or eternal existence of one's own identity or self, because it is grasping at permanence that forces us to cling on to this very 'now-ness' or matters of one's lifetime alone. By releasing the grip of this grasping and enduring within us, we will be in a better position to appreciate the value of working for our future lifetimes.

113

Whether one accepts rebirth or not, for a religious person the most important point at the time of death is to stop the flow of thoughts in our gross consciousness by invoking clearly one's faith in God or any other positive mental state. Ideally, one should keep one's mind as clear as possible and avoid anything that can cloud it. Nevertheless, if the dying person is in great pain and there is nothing that inspires them with a positive outlook, it is preferable not to die in a fully aware state. In such a case, it is helpful to give tranquillizers or medication.

114

For those who have no religion or spiritual path, and whose attitude and outlook is very far from being a religious one, the most important point at the moment of death is to be calm and relaxed, and to keep clearly in mind that death is a natural process that is part of life.

115

*I*f you are taking care of someone who is dying, try to adopt the attitude that is best suited to their personality, to the nature of their illness, to whether or not they have religious beliefs and to whether or not they believe in rebirth. Do everything in your power to help the dying person relax by creating a peaceful atmosphere around him. If you are agitated, he or she will be disturbed by many thoughts and feel uncomfortable. In Buddhist terms, there is a danger that you might provoke negative tendencies in him.

116

If a dying person follows the same religion as you, then remind them of the practices they are familiar with, or help to rekindle their faith. At the time of death, the mind becomes less clear. It would be useless to encourage a dying person to practise something new or something that he is not used to. Once the gross consciousness has dissolved and the arising of the subtle consciousness has begun, the only thing that can help us is the strength of our spiritual training and the power of positive thoughts.

117

*I*n cases when a person is in a coma, and when only the breathing continues without awareness, if it is impossible to bring the person around then you need to act accordingly. If the family is well off and cares for the dying person to the extent of wanting to do anything to keep them alive, even an extra day, then it is important to try to do this. Even if this does not help the dying person at all, it will fulfil the wishes of their loved ones.

When there is no hope left that the person will regain consciousness, or when such hope is unrealistic because what is required to bring this about is too expensive, would impoverish the family or create serious problems for other people, then it is best simply to say 'goodbye'.

118

According to Buddhism, although one should do one's utmost to reduce a person's suffering, nevertheless the truth remains that nobody can escape the suffering they have generated through their own actions. In other words, one suffers as a result of one's own actions (or karma), and the effect of one's actions is inescapable. If the person were dying in a place where there were no physical comforts whatsoever, or in another form of existence where nobody could take care of him, his suffering would be far worse. Since there are people to care for him now, it is preferable for him to suffer in his present body.

MEDITATIONS ON WORKING HARD AND HAVING LITTLE SPARE TIME

119

I call some of my friends 'slaves to money'. Without taking a moment's rest, they exhaust themselves running here and there; they are forever leaving for Japan, for the United States, for Korea, and do not dare take any holiday.

Naturally, if their activities are devoted to benefiting others or to developing their country, one can only rejoice at such an effort. Those who have noble goals and who work night and day to realize them deserve our praise. But even in these cases, it is good to take a rest from time to time to preserve one's health. It is better to be useful over a longer period, and at a moderate pace, than to make inordinate efforts that are short-lived.

120

If frantic activity is aimed at satisfying one's personal ambitions, and if in the process one exhausts oneself and ruins one's health, this is tantamount to destroying oneself for nothing.

Meditations on Prison and Prisoners

121

People who commit crimes are imprisoned and excluded from society. They then consider they are bad and that the community has rejected them. Without any hope of bettering themselves or starting a new life, they behave violently towards their fellow prisoners and abuse the weakest ones. In such conditions there is little chance they will improve.

122

I sometimes reflect on the fact that when a general kills thousands of people he is called a hero. His actions are called extraordinary and he is widely praised. But if someone who is completely lost kills another human being, he is treated as a murderer, put into prison or even executed.

123

Some people make fortunes dishonestly and are never caught. Others steal a few notes out of desperation and they are dragged into prison in handcuffs.

124

We are all potential criminals, and those who we put into prison are no worse, deep down, than any one of us. They have succumbed to ignorance, desire and anger, ailments that we all suffer from but to different degrees. Our duty is to help them recover.

125

Society should not reject those who have committed mistakes and who are branded criminals. They are fully-fledged human beings who are members of society just as we are, and they, too, can change. It is imperative to give them back hope and the will to take a new direction in life.

126

I have visited a prison in Delhi Tihar, in India, where a prison governor named Kirian Bedi looks after the prisoners very humanely. She provides them with a certain spiritual education, teaches them meditation and instils them with a peace of mind which frees them from feelings of guilt. The prisoners are happy to find that they are loved and cared for. After a while, even before their release, they become satisfied, they trust in human values and are able to re-integrate into society. For me, this is a very good example of the way we should go.

127

The case of young delinquents is especially sad. Firstly, because their lives have hardly started and are already wasted. And then, because this sort of tragedy often occurs through lack of experience, in difficult social conditions, at a time when one has not had the chance to ask oneself how one can stand on one's own feet.

128

The main advice I would give young delinquents, and all those in prison, is never to lose heart, never to lose hope, and to try to improve oneself. Always say to yourself: 'I recognize my mistake, I will not do it again, I will behave well, I will be helpful to others.' We are all capable of changing. We all have the same type of brain and the same potential. We can never say that we are a hopeless case, other than through ignorance or as a passing thought.

129

Poor prisoners! They committed crimes because they suddenly fell under the power of their negative emotions, and there they are, excluded from society, with nothing to hope for in this life.

Meditations on Homosexuality

130

Many people have asked me what I think of homosexuality. For believers, the best thing is to decide what you should or should not do in accordance with your faith. Certain Christians say that homosexuality is a serious fault, and others do not. Certain Buddhists accept it whereas others believe that it is practically the same as giving up being a Buddhist.

According to the Buddhist scriptures, there are ten harmful acts we should avoid and sexual misconduct is one of these.[2] By this we mean above all taking another person's partner, but it also includes homosexuality, oral sex, anal sex and masturbation. This does not mean that practising such things prevents you from being a Buddhist. Apart from erroneous views – that is, believing that the laws of moral causation do

2. The other nine are: killing, stealing, slander, lying, harmful speech, gossip, envy, harmful intentions, and erroneous views.

not exist – none of the ten harmful actions, not even killing, entails that one cannot be a Buddhist. Anyone who kills another human being certainly commits a very harmful act. If he is a monk and if he tries to conceal his crime, he breaks his vows irremediably and ceases to be a member of the monastic community. But he can continue to practise his faith.

131

*I*f you are not a religious believer and wish to have a sexual relationship with someone of the same sex, with mutual consent, without there being rape or abuse of any kind, and if you find in this a non-violent satisfaction, there is nothing I can say against it. I even think, and this is an important point, that it is unfair for homosexuals to be rejected by society, as they sometimes are, or to be punished and lose their jobs. We cannot place them on the same level as criminals.

132

I think that in terms of Buddhism generally, homosexuality is a fault in relation to certain precepts but it is not harmful in itself unlike rape, or killing, or other actions which cause others to suffer. The same applies to masturbation. That is why there is no reason to reject homosexuals or to discriminate against them.

I would add that neither is it fair systematically to despise religions that condemn sexual misconduct, simply because this does not correspond with our own way of thinking or behaving. Before we criticize any rule, it is good to try and understand the true reasons behind it.

Meditations on Politics

133

Politicians often make many promises in order to attract the respect and support of electors. 'I will do this, I will do that, just wait and see.' But if they want to be respected and supported, it is more important, in my opinion, that they should be honest and express genuine convictions.

134

*I*f our words simply change according to circumstance, people notice and they will remember: 'Before he said that and now he is saying this. So which is true?' Sincerity is an essential quality. Especially these days, when the media are chasing after everything people say and do, it is even more important than in the past that one keeps to one's convictions and expresses them whatever the circumstances.

135

If we always speak frankly, those who like our ideas will appreciate them and will rally to us. If, on the other hand, we behave in an opportunistic way and make all sorts of promises in front of the media which we then treat as irrelevant once elected, that is a bad strategy. Not only is it not ethical, but on a practical level it is foolish. At the next election it will go against us. What is the point of making so much effort if it only gets us elected once?

136

*O*nce we are in power, we must be particularly mindful of what we do, but also of what we think. When one is a president, a minister or in another powerful position, one is escorted everywhere, honoured, surrounded by all sorts of comforts, and our influence is considerable. That is the time when we must pay special attention to our thoughts and motivation if we do not want to lose sight of our true goal. The more one is surrounded by bodyguards, the more one needs to strengthen the defences against one's own mind.

137

Before they are elected, some politicians have perfectly pure intentions. But once they are in post, they grow full of themselves and completely forget their original aim. They see themselves as good people, protecting the electorate and playing an indispensable role. And they think that in return they can do what they fancy and that nobody has the right to comment. Even if they commit reprehensible actions, they persuade themselves that these are not really serious compared with the devotion they have for their job. In this way, they can become easily corrupted. When we have strength and power, we should be doubly careful.

138

People nowadays have little faith in politicians. This is sad. They say that politics is a dirty game. In fact, it is not dirty in itself; human beings make it so. In the same way, we cannot say that religion is evil by nature, but certain corrupt priests may degrade it by abusing people's faith. Politics becomes dirty when politicians behave immorally. Everyone loses out because every society needs politicians. Especially in democracies, it is essential to have a number of parties, some in power and others in opposition, and therefore it is necessary to have politicians and parties that are worthy of respect.

139

*I*n defence of politicians, they are necessarily the products of a society. If it is a society that thinks only of money and power, without any concern for moral values, we should not be surprised if politicians are corrupt, and should not therefore consider that the responsibility for such a situation lies entirely with them.

Meditations on the Legal System

140

*I*n any society, it is necessary to follow a certain number of rules. Those who commit crimes or harmful acts must be punished and those who behave well should be encouraged. The system can only function well thanks to laws and to those who apply them. If the guardians of justice and morality have no integrity themselves, the system becomes unjust. Is this not exactly what one often sees in some countries, where the rich and powerful are not brought to justice or they win their cases easily, while the poor are given heavy punishments? This is sad.

141

*O*nly yesterday, someone was telling me that in the United States judges are either pro-abortion or anti-abortion without anything in-between. And yet, between having an abortion for serious reasons – for example, if the mother's life is threatened and one has to choose between her life and the baby's – and having an abortion because the birth of a child would prevent us from going on holiday or buying new furniture, there is an appreciable difference. But in the view of these judges, there apparently is no difference. It would be good to study this subject in detail so we could define specific cases and state clearly: in such and such a case, abortion is prohibited, and in another case it is allowed.

142

*I*n Argentina recently, a judge asked me what I think of the death penalty as a means of upholding the law. My position is that the death penalty is unacceptable for a variety of reasons and I sincerely hope that one day it will be abolished throughout the world. Most importantly, it is a very serious act that takes away from the criminal any chance of redeeming himself. And yet criminals are human beings like any other, who can improve according to circumstance in the same way as you or I could, in certain circumstances, become worse. Let us give them a chance. Let us not treat them as an evil that we want to get rid of at all costs.

143

When our body is sick we do not destroy it, we try to heal it. Why should we destroy the harmful elements of society rather than taking care of them?

144

I put a question to a judge: 'Suppose two men have committed the same crime and are condemned to life imprisonment. One is single, but the other has several young children and happens to be their only parent, as their mother has died. If you put the second in prison, the children will have nobody to look after them. What do you do?'

The judge replied that according to the law, the two men must receive the same sentence. Society will be responsible for bringing up the children.

I could not help thinking that while, from the point of view of the action that has been committed, it is quite normal that both men should be given the same sentence, from the point of view of the circumstances in which that sentence is to be applied there is a tremendous difference between the two cases. By punishing the father, one will also be punishing the children most cruelly and they did nothing wrong. The judge told me that the law has not anticipated any answer to such a problem.

Meditations on the Future of the World

145

A handful of intellectuals and religious people, and a large number of scientists, have become aware of the acute problems that the world currently faces: the environment, wars, famines, the suffering of large numbers of people, the enormous gap between rich and poor nations. The problem is that they just express their point of view and leave the responsibility for taking action on the ground to a small number of organizations.

In fact, we should all be concerned and we are all responsible. This is also one of the meanings of democracy, I think. Each one of us should act on our level, cooperate with others, discuss the problems, exhort those responsible to act positively, firmly criticize any disastrous policies and take our case to the United Nations and national governments. In this way, the influence we can wield will certainly be more effective.

146

A few people take me for a kind of prophet. I am merely speaking on behalf of the countless human beings who are suffering from poverty, wars, arms merchants, and so on, and who do not have the power to express themselves. I am just a spokesperson. I have no yearning for power and no intention of taking on the rest of the world.

It is not appropriate for an isolated Tibetan, from a far-off land, to assume an extraordinary responsibility and take on such a struggle. It would be stupid. At my age, anyway, it is time to retire.

But I will remain unshakeable in my commitment until the moment of my death, even if I have to attend conferences in a wheelchair!

Meditations on Education

147

I am convinced that the progress or decline of humanity rests very largely with educators and teachers, who therefore have a tremendous responsibility.

148

If you are a teacher, try not to merely transmit knowledge, but try at the same time to awaken your students' minds to basic human qualities such as kindness, compassion, forgiveness, and understanding. Do not communicate these as though they were the reserve of ethics or religion. Show them that these qualities are indispensable for the happiness and survival of everyone.

149

*T*each students to debate and to resolve conflicts in a non-violent way; and as soon as there is a disagreement, teach them to take interest in what the other person thinks. Teach them not to view things in a narrow-minded way; not to think only of themselves, their community, their country, or their race, but to realize that all beings have the same rights and the same needs. Make them aware of our universal responsibility; show them that whatever we do matters, and that everything has an effect on the rest of the world.

150

Do not limit yourself to words; set your students an example.
Then they will remember what you tell them better.
Be responsible for your students' future in all its guises.

Meditations on Science and Technology

151

If there are certain fields of science or technology where discoveries do not have major consequences, this is not the case in others, such as genetics or nuclear physics, where their application can be either extremely beneficial or extremely harmful. It would be preferable that scientists working in these disciplines felt a sense of responsibility for the work they do and did not shut their eyes to the potential disasters it might bring about.

152

Specialists often have too narrow a field of vision. They are not sufficiently concerned about relating their research to a broader context. I am not saying that their intentions are bad, but by devoting themselves solely to the exhaustive study of one particular area, they do not have time to reflect on the long-term effect of their discoveries. I admire Einstein, who warned others about the possible dangers involved in research on nuclear fission.

153

Scientists should always bear in mind the need not to harm. I am thinking in particular about genetics and its potential deviations. The fact that one day we might be able to clone individuals whose only reason for living is as a source of spare parts for others, seems utterly terrifying. In the same way, I would condemn the use of human foetuses for research purposes and, as a Buddhist, I would also have to condemn vivisection and all other cruel practices carried out on any living being, even if this is done in the name of research. How can we deny the right not to suffer to a whole class of beings when we uphold it so fiercely for ourselves?

MEDITATIONS ON COMMERCE AND BUSINESS

154

Generally, I tell men and women engaged in business that there is nothing wrong with having a competitive spirit if this means that you say to yourself: 'I want to give the best of myself, I want to reach the top like others.' On the other hand, in order to get to the top it is not permissible to prevent others from succeeding by means of base methods such as deceiving them, slandering them, or sometimes even by killing them.

155

We should consider that our competitors are also human beings and have the same rights and needs as ourselves. We should think that they too are members of our society. It is all the better if they are also successful.

156

The only aggressive attitude that is acceptable is recognizing one's own talent and working with unshakeable determination, saying to oneself, 'I, too, am capable and even if nobody helps me, I will succeed.'

MEDITATIONS ON WRITING AND JOURNALISM

157

Writers and journalists are very influential in society. Even if human life is short-lived, written texts can survive for centuries. In Buddhism, for example, it is because the teachings of Buddha, of Shantideva and other great masters have been put into writing that they have been able to teach people for so long about love, compassion and the altruistic attitude of the enlightened mind; and this is why we can still study them today. Unfortunately, other texts have been at the root of tremendous suffering, such as those which spread the extreme ideologies of fascism and communism. Indirectly, writers have the power to create the happiness or the unhappiness of millions of beings.

158

What I generally say to journalists is this: at this juncture, especially in democratic countries, your power over public opinion is immense and so is your responsibility. One of your most useful tasks, in my view, is to combat lies and corruption. Examine in detail the behaviour of the heads of state, honestly and impartially, as well as that of ministers and other powerful personalities. When the scandal about President Clinton's sex life broke, I greatly appreciated the fact that the head of the most powerful nation in the world could be brought to court just like any other citizen.

159

*I*t is an excellent thing that journalists investigate and inquire into the lives of people in public life in order to show whether or not the electorate should consider them trustworthy. But it is important to carry out such inquiries honestly, without deception or bias. Your aim should not be to ensure that your own side wins by demolishing the reputation of a political rival or an opposition party.

160

Journalists ought to emphasize and promote fundamental human values. Usually they are only interested in hot stories, especially if they are awful. Deep down, human beings consider murder unacceptable and shocking, as something that should never happen. That is why, whenever it occurs, it makes front-page news. The same goes for corruption and other malpractice. By contrast, we consider it completely normal to bring up our children, look after old people and care for the sick, and do not think that people who do these things deserve to figure in the news.

161

There is a risk that we end up thinking that humans are cruel by nature and that there is no way we can prevent this cruelty from expressing itself. One day, if we are firmly convinced of this, then we will no longer have any hope in the future of humankind. Maybe we will say to ourselves: 'Since it is impossible to cultivate human qualities and to promote peace, why not become a terrorist? Since helping others is pointless, why not ignore the rest of the world and live just for oneself, on the margins?'

If you are a journalist, try to be aware of this problem and take your responsibility seriously. Even if your readers or listeners do not crave for it, tell them about people who are doing good things, too.

Meditations on Farming and the Environment

162

Farmers play a crucial role in protecting or degrading both the environment and human health. At the present time, what with the pollution of aquifers, the abuse of chemical fertilizers and pesticides, and other problems that are regularly brought to our attention, one is becoming increasingly aware of the responsibility human beings have for environmental degradation and other such problems. Mad cow disease is a particularly striking example of this, since it is due to the use of animal products in the feed. Logically, those responsible should be punished, but, apparently, nobody is commenting on this. And yet hundreds of cows are killed, and they are only the victims of human actions.

163

I think we should make much less use of chemicals in farming and, as far as possible, keep in harmony with natural processes. In the immediate term, this may reduce profits, but in the long run it would be beneficial. It would also be good to reduce the size and the number of industrially reared herds as these are environmentally harmful. Unnatural animal feeds also have unpredictable effects, as we are now discovering. When one thinks of the waste of time, money and energy, and of the useless suffering they cause, one cannot help thinking it would be wiser to use different methods.

164

All sentient beings have the right to life. It is obvious that mammals, birds and fish all feel pleasure and pain, and that therefore they do not like pain any more than we do. When we abuse animals simply for a profit motive, even if we leave the Buddhist point of view aside, such action contradicts elementary moral values.

165

From the point of view of conflicts and differences, of all the various species of animal on the planet, human beings are the biggest troublemakers. That is clear. I imagine that if there were no longer any humans on the planet, the planet itself would be much safer. Certainly millions of fish, chickens, and other small animals might enjoy some sort of genuine liberation!

166

Whoever lacks the slightest hesitation and the slightest compassion in killing animals or making them suffer will logically find it more difficult than most to feel compassion for their relatives. It is always dangerous to ignore the suffering of any living being, of whatever species, even if we think it necessary to sacrifice an animal for the benefit of the majority. To deny the suffering involved, or to avoid thinking about it, is a convenient solution, but such an attitude opens the door to all kinds of excesses as we witness in wartime. It also destroys our own happiness. As I often say, sympathy and compassion always end up proving beneficial.

167

Some people remark that animals eat each other anyway. That is true, but we cannot deny that animals that eat other animals do so in a simple and direct fashion: when they are hungry, they kill, when they are not hungry, they do not kill. This is a far cry from the attitude of human beings, who slaughter millions of cows, sheep, chickens, and so on, just for profit.

I met a Polish Jew one day, a good and intelligent man. As he was a vegetarian and Tibetans are not, he asked: 'I do not eat animals, but if I did eat them I would have the courage to kill them myself.' Us Tibetans get other people to slaughter animals and then we eat them! [Laughs.]

MEDITATIONS ON WAR

168

In every human society there are people who cause many problems, and it is necessary to put effective measures in place to prevent them from causing harm. When there is no other alternative, one may well have to decide to use armed force.

For me, an army should not serve to propagate a doctrine or invade another country, but only as a last resort to put an end to the actions of those who destroy the well-being of humanity and sow the seeds of chaos. The only acceptable goal of any war is the happiness of everyone involved, not personal interests. War is therefore a last resort.

169

*H*istory shows us that violence only engenders more violence and rarely solves problems. On the other hand, it certainly creates unfathomable suffering. It is also apparent that even when war seems wise and logical as a means to end a conflict, we can never know for sure whether by putting out a fire we are in fact lighting a furnace.

170

Today, war has become cold and inhumane. Modern weaponry enables us to kill thousands of people without risking one's own life or witnessing the suffering one has caused. Those who give the order to kill are often thousands of miles away from the battlefield. And those who are innocent, the women and children who just wish to stay alive, are those who are killed or mutilated. One could almost feel nostalgic about the way wars used to be, when the lord would march out at the head of his troops; his death generally meant the end of the conflict. At least we should restore the human dimension of war.

171

As soon as men have weapons they tend to use them. My view is that there should no longer be any national armies. The world should be demilitarised, apart from a multinational force that would intervene only when certain elements were threatening the peace of a particular region.

172

Everyone talks about peace, but peace is impossible to bring about externally if one harbours anger or hatred within. Neither can the wish for peace be reconciled with the arms race. Nuclear weapons are considered a deterrent, but in the long term this does not seem to me to be a very sensible or effective strategy.

173

Certain countries spend colossal sums on developing arms. So much money, energy, and talent is wasted, while the threat of things going wrong only produces more and more fear.

174

*I*t is up to everyone to bring an end to war. We can of course identify those who have incited conflict, but we cannot pretend that they sprung up out of nowhere or that they acted in isolation. They were members of a society of which we are all members too, and for which each one of us carries a share of responsibility. If we want to bring about peace in the world, let us start by creating it in ourselves.

175

Peace in the world depends on peace of mind, and peace of mind depends on an awareness that all human beings are members of a single family, despite the variety of beliefs, ideologies, and political and economic systems. These are mere details compared to what brings us together. The most important thing is that we are all human beings, living on the same small planet. We all need to cooperate with each other, both individually and between states, if only to ensure our survival.

Meditations on dedicating one's life to others

Those who dedicate their lives to others in terms of health, education, spiritual life, family or social life or in any other field, gladden my heart. Every human society generates its burden of problems and suffering. To do whatever is possible to resolve such difficulties is certainly worthy of praise.

From the Buddhist point of view, it is important not to help someone simply out of duty or pleasure – in the way some people like gardening, for example. If one acts out of love and compassion, with a smile and a few friendly words, one will definitely give happiness to others. The action itself may seem the same, but its benefits will be infinitely greater.

177

*I*f you are a doctor, don't look after your patients out of routine or obligation. Your patients might get the impression that nobody is really taking care of them, that they are not being examined with enough care or that they are being treated as guinea pigs. Some surgeons have performed so many operations that they end up seeing all their patients as machines that are to be repaired, and are no longer aware they are dealing with human beings. By losing sight of the human being as the object of our kindness and compassion, they cut people open, replace organs, and sew them up again in the same way one handles the spare parts of a car or pieces of wood.

178

When we take care of others it is extremely important to cultivate an altruistic attitude. This benefits not only the person on the receiving end, but also the person who gives.

179

The more we are concerned about the happiness of others, the more we are building our own happiness at the same time. But never think about this when you are actually giving. Do not expect anything in return; think only of what is good for the other person.

180

Never consider yourself to be superior to those you are helping. Whether you give them your money, your time or your energy, always act with humility even if the other person is dirty, shifty, stupid, or clothed in rags. Personally, whenever I come across a beggar, I always try not to view him as inferior but as a human being who is no different from me.

181

When you help someone, do not be content with solving their immediate problems by giving money, for example. Give them also the means to resolve their problems themselves.

182

I think that every human being has an innate sense of 'I'. We cannot explain why that feeling is there, but it is. Along with it comes a desire for happiness and a wish to overcome suffering. This is quite justified: we have a natural right to achieve as much happiness as possible, and we also have a right to overcome suffering. The whole of human history has developed on the basis of this feeling. In fact, it is not limited to human beings; from the Buddhist point of view, even the tiniest insect has this feeling and, according to its capacity, is trying to gain some happiness and avoid unhappy situations.

183

There are several ways of being happy. Some people are slightly disturbed and in a perpetual state of dumb bliss. They always think everything is fine. That is not the kind of happiness we are dealing with here.

Others base their happiness on the possession of material goods and the satisfaction of the senses. We have already noted how fragile such happiness is. Even when you think you are really happy, if you take that happiness for granted you will doubly suffer when circumstances are no longer in your favour.

Yet others believe that their happiness is due to moral attitudes and behaviour. This is the kind of happiness we need, because it is based on profound causes and does not depend on circumstance.

184

*I*f your attitude is not right, then even if you are surrounded by good friends and the best facilities, you cannot be happy. This is why mental attitude is more important than external conditions. Despite this, it seems to me that many people are more concerned about their external conditions and neglect the inner attitude of mind. I suggest that we should pay more attention to our inner qualities.

185

*I*n order to have lasting happiness, we first need to acknowledge the reality of suffering. This may be depressing to begin with, but it works in the long run. Although some people prefer to avoid facing reality by taking drugs, by seeking false states of bliss through directionless spiritual paths, or by living life in the fast lane so they have no time to think deeply, they only experience a short reprieve. When their problems come back in force they find themselves at sea and 'fill the land with lamentations', as we say in Tibet. Anger or despair takes them over, compounding their initial difficulty with pointless suffering.

186

Try to understand where our suffering comes from. Like everything else, it is the result of a countless number of causes and conditions. If our feelings depended on one cause alone, we would only have to meet one cause of happiness for happiness to arise systematically. But we know very well that this is not how things work. So let's give up the idea that there is always one thing that is responsible for our unhappiness, and that if we could identify it we would not suffer.

187

We need to recognize that suffering is part of life or, in Buddhist terms, of samsara, the cycle of conditioned existence. If we regard suffering as negative and abnormal, and consider ourselves its victims, then life becomes a misery. Our attitude is the problem. Happiness is possible only when what we call suffering no longer causes us distress.

188

According to Buddhism, reflecting on the reality of suffering never induces either pessimism or despair. It leads to the discovery of the root causes of our plight: desire, hatred and ignorance, and to a way of freeing ourselves from them. By 'ignorance' we mean not understanding the true nature of people and things. It gives rise to the other two poisons. When ignorance dissolves, desire and hatred have no foundation and the source of our suffering has dried up. As a result, we experience a happiness that is spontaneously altruistic and that is no longer at the mercy of negative emotions.

MEDITATIONS ON UNHAPPINESS

189

*I*n industrialized countries, one sees many unhappy people. They have everything they need, enjoy all the conditions required for a comfortable life, and yet they are not content with their lot. They make themselves unhappy through jealousy or for all sorts of other reasons. Certain people are continually on the alert for a cataclysm, while others believe the end of the world is nigh. Such people manufacture their own suffering because they are unable to think sanely. If only they changed their way of seeing things, their torment would disappear.

190

There are many people who have real reasons to suffer, who are really ill, for example, on the breadline, disaster victims, or abused. And yet, here again, they often have the power to remedy this. Practically speaking, they can and should take care of themselves, speak out against their abusers and take them to court demanding damages, or again they can work extremely hard if they do not have enough food or clothes. And mentally, they can adopt a positive attitude.

191

*I*t is our mental attitude that determines the degree of our suffering. If one is sick, for example, the only useful reaction is to do whatever is possible to get better: see a doctor, follow a treatment, do certain exercises, and so on. But, generally, we complicate our situation by worrying about it, adding mental anguish to our physical suffering.

192

*I*f we have a serious illness, we often see it in the most negative way possible. If we have a head injury, we think to ourselves, 'This is really the worst thing that could have happened to me. If only it were a problem with my legs!' Instead of telling ourselves that thousands of others are suffering at least as much as we are, we feel sorry for ourselves as if we were the only person in the world to experience suffering.

And yet it is possible to adopt the reverse attitude and to think, if our arms are paralysed, 'I can no longer use my arms, but at least my legs can still support me.' And if it's our legs, 'My legs will no longer carry me, but I can get around in a wheelchair and I can still write with my hands.' Simple thoughts like these are enough to bring comfort.

193

Whatever your situation it is always possible to view it in a positive light, especially nowadays when modern technology gives us more reason to have hope. It is impossible not to find any way of changing our outlook to reduce suffering that has been caused by external circumstances. It is very rare to find a case where we only have reasons to suffer with no possibility of reassurance. When you are faced with physical pain think of the positive side, keep this in mind and it will certainly help to relieve your sadness.

194

Even if you suffer from a serious long-term condition, there is definitely a way of not falling into despair. If you are a Buddhist, tell yourself: 'May this sickness purify my past negative actions. May I also take on the suffering of others, and go through it in their place.' Consider that countless beings are suffering just like you and pray that your suffering may help to appease theirs. If you do not have the strength to reflect in this way, the simple fact of being aware that you are not alone and that many others are in the same situation will help you to bear your hardship.

If you are a Christian and you have faith in God as creator of the universe, comfort yourself by thinking, 'I have not wanted this suffering, but there must be a reason for it since God, in his compassion, has given me life.'

If you do not have any religious faith, you can think that however terrible your misfortune, you are not the only one to suffer in this way. Even if you have no belief, try to imagine, above the area of your pain, a vivid light that pervades and dissolves your pain, and see if that helps.

195

Certain types of suffering come suddenly and inescapably, like the death of a loved one. In this case, of course, there is no question of trying to alter its cause. Nothing can be done in this respect. And this is precisely why you should consider that despair is pointless and only aggravates our sadness. Here, I am thinking especially of those who have no religious beliefs.

196

*I*t is important to examine our suffering, to find out where it has come from and if possible to cause it to dissolve. Usually, we do not think we have any share of responsibility in bringing about our own problems. Invariably, they are blamed on someone or something else. But I doubt that this is always the case. We are a bit like students who have failed an exam and who refuse to admit that if they had worked harder they would have been able to pass it. We get angry at so-and-so or proclaim that circumstances conspired against us. But don't things become even worse when this mental suffering is added to the initial difficulty?

197

The many conflicts within the human family and within one's own family, not to mention the conflicts within the community and between nations, as well as the internal conflicts within the individual – all conflicts and contradictions arise from the different ideas and views our intelligence brings. So, unfortunately, intelligence can sometimes create a quite unhappy state of mind. In this sense, intelligence becomes another source of human misery. Yet, at the same time, I think that, ultimately, intelligence is the tool with which we can overcome all these conflicts and differences.

198

Even if you lose someone very close, such as your father or mother, you should reason with yourself. After a certain age, life naturally draws to an end. When you were small, your parents did their utmost to bring you up. Now you have nothing to regret. Of course, if they die prematurely in a road accident, for example, the sadness is much greater.

Meditations on Pessimism

199

What I feel like saying to pessimists and perpetual worriers is this: how stupid you are! One day, in the United States, I met a woman who was very unhappy for no good reason. I said to her, 'Don't make yourself miserable. You are young, you still have many years to live, you have no reason to distress yourself.' She asked me why I didn't mind my own business. I felt sad. I answered that there was no point in saying that. I took her hand, gave her a friendly pat, and then her attitude changed.

We can only help people who feel this way through love and affection. Not with a superficial love or with words that are hollow, but with something that comes from the heart. When we discuss these things we are appealing to reason, but when we manifest genuine love and kindness we communicate directly with the other person. In the end this woman changed and she began to laugh heartily.

200

If you are disposed to pessimism, remember that you are part of human society and that deep down human beings naturally feel love for each other. You will always find someone in whom you can place your hope, someone who is worthy of being an example. Worrying will not get you anywhere.

201

Transform your thoughts into positive ones. It is a mistake to think that everyone is bad. Some people are wicked, that's true, but that does not mean everyone is. There are also many people who have a noble and generous spirit.

202

People who see the world pessimistically trust in no one and feel very isolated. But, fundamentally, the reason they feel lonely is because they do not think enough of others. When we do not think enough of others we judge them in relation to ourselves and imagine that they see us in the same light as we see them. It is not surprising that we feel lonely.

203

One day, a man came to Dharamsala who had very good relations with Communist China. On hearing of his arrival, many of the people here had branded him a 'Chinese Communist' and blackened his image even before setting eyes on him. As a result, when I first met him there was an uncomfortable atmosphere.

I had nothing against him personally; I viewed him as a human being like any other and thought that if he believed the Chinese it was simply because he was inadequately informed. The Tibetan situation was really tragic, and I was not going to tell him the opposite just to please him. I was going to tell him things as they are.

As soon as we met he spoke with a polemical tone, but I considered him simply as a human being and I spoke to him of Tibet in a friendly way. On the second day, his attitude had completely changed.

At the beginning, the confrontation made him

uncomfortable. If I had shown any nervousness too, both of us would have gradually become more and more entrenched behind our positions. I would not have listened to his arguments and he would have paid no heed to mine. But by considering him as a human being and thinking that all human beings are equal if sometimes ill-informed, and by behaving in a friendly way, I was slowly able to get him to open up.

204

There are people who only see the dark side of things. It's quite surprising. In the Tibetan community in exile, for example, we are all refugees sharing the same situation, but amongst us there are those who are always happy and who only talk of pleasant things which give cause for hope, and on the other hand there are those who see no good side to anything. They speak badly of everything and are continually anxious.

205

*I*t is said in the Buddhist scriptures, the world can appear as friend or foe, full of defects or full of qualities: it all depends on our mind. Generally, there is nothing that has only advantages or only disadvantages. Everything we use – food, clothes, buildings and so on – and all the people we live with – family, friends, superiors, inferiors, masters, disciples, and so forth – have both qualities and defects. That is how it is. In order to judge reality correctly, we must acknowledge the good and bad sides for what they are.

206

From a certain point of view, we can see everything in a positive light. Even suffering can be considered beneficial. I am simply saying that those who have been through a lot of hardship do not generally complain at small difficulties. The hardships they have experienced have forged their temperament and given them a broader perspective, a more stable mind, one that is closer to reality and more capable of seeing things as they are. By contrast, those who never see anything as a problem and spend their lives in cotton wool are dislocated from reality. Faced with a minor nuisance, they 'fill the land with lamentations'.

207

I have lost my country, I have spent the greater part of my life in exile, my people have been tortured and massacred, our temples have been flattened, our civilization destroyed, our country ransacked and its resources pillaged. None of this gives any cause for jubilation. Yet, at the same time, I have been greatly enriched through contact with other nations, other religions, other cultures, and other bodies of knowledge. I have discovered different forms of freedom and world-views that I did not know before.

208

Within the Tibetan community in exile, it is often those who have suffered the most who are the most joyful and the sturdiest emotionally. Having spent twenty years in prison in deplorable conditions, many individuals have told me that from the spiritual point of view they had been the best years of their life. A monk from my monastery was cruelly tortured for years so he would renounce his faith. When he escaped to India, I asked him if he had been afraid. He replied, quite genuinely, that his only fear had been losing compassion for his torturers.

209

People in France, Germany, and Britain who lived through the Second World War and the difficult economic period immediately afterwards are not thrown by minor worries. They are content with their lot because they have been through far worse. By contrast, those who did not live through that war and who live happily as in a kindergarten are prone to moaning and almost faint at the slightest difficulty. Happiness is there but they do not recognize it.

210

Some young people are not satisfied with material progress and turn to spirituality, and this seems positive to me. But in any case, you should be aware that the world is made of good things and bad, and that what we take to be reality is to a large extent fabricated by our own minds.

Meditations on Fear

211

From the moment they wake up, some people are full of inexplicable fear and anguish. This feeling can have many causes. Sometimes, the person has been badly treated by their parents, or brothers and sisters, when they were small. Others have been sexually abused. They have been assaulted and they have difficulty talking about it. Gradually a kind of fear establishes itself and they feel uneasy in themselves.

When they manage to express what they have experienced, if there is someone who can help them to understand that it is all over, that the past is past, then they may have a chance to close that chapter of their life. In Tibet, we say that the only way to unblock a conch shell is by blowing into it.

212

When I was young I was always afraid of dark rooms. As time went by, the fear went. Also with regard to meeting people, the more your mind is closed, the greater the possibility of developing fear or feeling uncomfortable. The more open you are, the less uncomfortable you will feel. That is my experience. If I meet anyone, whether a great man, a beggar, or just an ordinary person, to me there is no difference. The most important thing is to smile and show a genuine human face.

213

*I*f you are afraid because you have no self-confidence and feel that nothing you do will ever succeed, stop a while to think it over. Try to see why you imagine you are a loser before you have even started. You won't find any really valid reason. The problem stems from your way of thinking, not from a real ineptitude.

214

Genuine compassion is based on the recognition that others have the right to happiness just like yourself. One aspect of this kind of compassion is a sense of caring responsibility. When we develop that kind of motivation, our self-confidence increases automatically. This in turn reduces fear and that serves as a basis for determination. If you are really determined right from the start to accomplish a difficult task, then even if you fail first time, second time, third time, it doesn't matter. You aim is very clear, so you will continue to make an effort.

215

An effective method to overcome fear is to shift one's concern from oneself to others. When we actually see the difficulties that other people face, our own seem less enormous. When we come to the aid of others, our confidence is boosted and our fear and anguish are lessened. It is, of course, necessary for our desire to help to be sincere. If the only reason we have for helping others is to free ourselves from our own predicament, it will bring us back inevitably to ourselves and our fears.

Meditations on Suicide

216

*I*t is difficult to talk of suicide. There are so many reasons for it. Some people are overwhelmed by fear and anguish; others by despair. Certain people kill themselves because their pride has been hurt by what others have or have not done. There are people who are convinced that they will never manage to achieve anything, and those who experience intense desire and kill themselves through anger when that desire is not satisfied. Some people allow themselves to drown in sorrow. And there are many other reasons besides.

217

Generally speaking, anyone who commits suicide is eliminating any possible solution to his or her problem. Even if one has encountered nothing but difficulties until that point, this is no proof that some day one will not find the means to resolve things.

218

Most suicides are committed at a time of extreme emotion. Human beings should not take such a radical decision merely out of anger, desire or anguish. By acting impulsively there is a high risk of making a mistake. Since we are capable of reflecting on things, we should wait to be calm and relaxed before committing such an irreparable act.

219

My tutor Trijang Rinpoche told me the story of a man from Kham province who was very unhappy and who had decided to throw himself into the Tsangpo River in Lhasa. He took with him a bottle of alcohol and told himself that he would jump once he had drunk the bottle. To begin with, he was overwhelmed with emotion. Once he reached the river's edge, he sat for a moment on the bank. As he was slow to make up his mind to jump in, he began to drink some alcohol. And as this failed to give him enough courage, he drank a little more. Finally, he walked home, with the empty bottle under his arm.

Meditations on Loneliness and Isolation

220

I learned from a recent poll that a majority of Americans admit that they suffer from loneliness and isolation. One quarter of adults admitted that they had felt deeply lonely during the previous fortnight and this phenomenon appears to be very widespread.

There are thousands of people on city streets and yet none of them looks at each other. If their eyes cross, they do not smile unless they are meeting formally. People sit next to each other in trains for hours on end but do not talk to each other. Isn't this strange?

221

My sense is that the experience of loneliness is due to two main causes. One is that people have become too numerous. When the world was less populated, we must have been more acutely aware of belonging to the human family, people definitely knew each other better, and the need for mutual support would have been greater. Even today, in small villages people know each other, lend their tools and machines and carry out heavy work together. In the old days, they would get together regularly, go to church and pray together. They had more opportunities to communicate.

Now that the world is overpopulated, millions of people are crowded into the big cities. Looking at them, one would think that their only concern is to work and earn a salary. Each individual seems to live a separate, independent life. Modern machines give us great autonomy and we have the impression, mistaken of course, that other people are less and less important for our well-being. This situation encourages indifference and a feeling of isolation.

222

Another cause behind the experience of isolation, in my view, is that in modern society we are all terribly busy. If we talk to someone, even if only to say 'How are you?' we feel we are losing two precious seconds of our life. We have hardly finished working before we dive into the newspaper. 'Let's see what the news is.' Discussing things with a friend is wasting time.

223

People who live in cities usually know quite a few people. One has to say hello. As there is a risk that one will be drawn into conversation with everyone, this isn't practical. So we avoid contact and if someone speaks to you it feels like an intrusion.

224

When people in a big town or city feel lonely, this does not mean that they lack human companions, but rather that they lack human affection. As a result of this, their mental health eventually becomes very poor. On the other hand, those people who grow up in an atmosphere of human affection have a much more positive and gentle development of their bodies, their minds, and behaviours.

225

Society is becoming less and less humane and our lives are growing mechanical. Each morning, we go out to work. When work is finished, we distract ourselves in a nightclub or similar. We get drunk, go home late, sleep for a few hours. And the next day, half asleep and in a daze, we go out to work again. Don't many people in cities spend much of their lives like this? And as each person has become rather like a cog in a machine, they follow the herd whether they feel like it or not. After a while this lifestyle becomes hard to sustain and we close up in indifference.

226

Don't go out and drink too much in the evening. Once your working day is over, it would be better to go home. Take your time to eat, have a cup of tea or something, read a book, relax, and go to bed. Get up early next morning. If you go to work with a fresh and open mind, I think your life will be quite different.

227

Everyone knows that feeling isolated is neither useful nor pleasant. Each one of us has to struggle against it. But as it arises from a great number of causes and conditions, it is important to tackle it in the early stages. The family, that fundamental unit of society, should become a place where one feels happy and where one can develop in an atmosphere of love and affection.

228

If you feel hatred and ill-feeling toward others, they may feel similarly toward you and, as a result, suspicion and fear will create a distance between you and make you feel lonely and isolated. Not all members of your community will have similar negative feelings toward you, but some may look on you negatively because of your own feelings.

229

*I*f children are brought up in a warm and caring environment, both at home and at school, once they are adult and socially engaged they will be capable of helping others. When they meet someone for the first time they will feel at ease and won't be afraid to speak to them. They will contribute to the creation of a new atmosphere in which the feeling of isolation will be much less common.

MEDITATIONS ON ANGER

230

When we find ourselves under the domination of anger or hatred, we do not feel right, either mentally or physically. Everyone else notices this and nobody feels like being with us. Even animals run away from us, apart from fleas and mosquitoes which are only after our blood! We lose our appetite, we don't sleep well, sometimes we get ulcers, and if we are continually in this state, we certainly shorten our lifespan.

To what end? Even if we allow our rage to go all the way, we will never eliminate all our enemies. Do you know of anyone who ever has? As long as we harbour that inner enemy of anger or hatred, however successful we are at destroying our outer enemies today, others will emerge tomorrow.

231

*O*ur true enemies are the mental poisons of ignorance, hatred, desire, jealousy and pride. They are the only things that are capable of destroying our happiness. Anger and hatred, in particular, are at the root of much of the suffering in this world, from family quarrels to large-scale conflicts. They render any pleasant situation unbearable. No religion praises their virtues; they all emphasize love and kindness. We only have to read the many descriptions of paradise to realize that they are about peace, beauty, exquisite gardens, and flowers, but never, as far as I know, about conflicts and wars. So anger is not attributed any positive qualities.

232

*H*ow should we deal with anger? Some people believe there is nothing wrong with it. Those who are not accustomed to looking at their own minds think that emotions are an inherent part of their nature and that they should not be repressed but expressed. If this were true, we would also have to say that ignorance and illiteracy are also part of our nature, since when we are born we know nothing. And yet we do everything to eliminate them, and nobody claims that they are natural and shouldn't be changed. So why not do the same with hatred or anger, which are much more devastating? It is certainly worth a try.

233

*I*t takes time to learn anything, and it is impossible to know everything, yet it is good to become a little less ignorant. In the same way, it is difficult to get rid of anger for good, but if we do so to some extent, the result is worthwhile. You might, of course, want to argue that it is your affair and none of my business! [Laughs]

234

Psychologists may tell you not to repress a feeling like anger, but to externalise it. But they will not tell you to go looking for it or to develop it further. Train yourself to see the flaws in your anger, and even if you still think that it is an inherent part of your mental make-up, you will not be able to stop yourself from concluding that you would be better off without it.

235

Avoid as far as possible any situation that provokes you to violent reactions. If you react despite this, try not to get carried away. If you know someone who has the knack of irritating you, try to forget this unfortunate trait and look at the person from another angle.

236

The people who we consider our enemies have not been hostile to us from birth. They have become so as a result of certain types of thinking and behaviour. It is then that we call them 'enemies'. If the attitude they have towards us changes completely they become 'friends'. One and the same person could therefore be our 'enemy' one day and our 'friend' the next. This is absurd.

237

Try to discern clearly between the person and his or her attitude in the moment. Do not react against the person but against the emotion or mode of behaviour. Reject any wish to harm the person himself. Try to help him change and benefit him as much as possible. If you restrict yourself to trying to put a stop to his actions, there is a chance that he will cease quickly from acting as your enemy. He may even become your friend.

238

You do not have to put up with the harm inflicted on you or on others. Fight against it, but without any hatred for those who perpetrate it. Do not get angry at them and do not seek vengeance. In this way your reaction will not be a form of revenge, or an anger responding to another anger. This is what patience really is. It is difficult to react correctly when we are in a rage, so drop your rage.

239

Recently, when I was in Jerusalem, I participated in a debate between Israeli and Palestinian students. At the end, a Palestinian said that everything was fine right then, while they were in dialogue, but as soon as they were on the street it was different. When the Israeli police arrested them they would be furious and view the Israelis as their enemies. They were wondering what they should do. They discussed it a little and had the idea that they could consider the other as 'an image of God'. One of the students said, 'Each time you are in front of a man who has harmed you, whatever that harm has been, think that that person is an image of God and your anger will dissipate.' Isn't that a good idea?

240

Someone wrote to me saying that when he meditated, the image of the Dalai Lama came to him and helped him a lot. Now, when he gets angry, he thinks of me and his anger subsides. I am not sure that my photo has the power to pacify anger. [Laughs] Rather, I think that when anger rises suddenly within us, if instead of focusing on the object that is provoking it we think of someone or something that we love, our mind calms down, at least to a certain extent. For example, you can think of the man or woman you are in love with. This will distract your mind and, as we say, 'two thoughts cannot arise simultaneously'. Our mind automatically follows the direction of the new image if that is stronger, and the previous one disappears.

241

I often say that by giving in to anger, we are not necessarily harming our enemy but we are definitely harming ourselves. We lose our sense of inner peace, we do everything wrong, our digestion is bad, we cannot sleep well, we put off our guests or we cast furious glances at those who have the impudence of being in our way. If we have a pet, we forget to feed it. We make life impossible for those who live with us, and even our dearest friends are kept at a distance. Since there are fewer and fewer people who sympathize with us, we feel more and more lonely.

As for our supposed enemy, perhaps he is sitting quietly at home. If one day our neighbours tell him what they have seen or heard, he will rejoice. If he is told, 'He is really unhappy, he has lost his appetite, his complexion is pale, his hair is uncombed, he can't sleep, he is taking tranquillizers, nobody comes to visit him any more, even his dog is afraid to go near him and never stops barking', that person will be delighted. And if he learns that he has had to be taken to hospital, his satisfaction will have no bounds!

MEDITATIONS ON DESIRE

242

The aim of desire is to be satisfied. If it dominates us and we are always craving for more, that goal is never reached and instead of finding happiness we only get suffering. These days we talk a lot about sexual freedom. But when one gives in to sexual desire without any restraint, merely for pleasure, one does not find any lasting satisfaction and creates a host of problems of which the negative consequences – the suffering of an abandoned partner, relationship break-ups, children's lives turned upside down, venereal diseases, AIDS – are quite disproportionate to the brief moments of pleasure one may have experienced.

243

*I*t is the very nature of desire to rise again ever more strongly, even after one thinks it has been satisfied. Whoever allows him or herself to be trapped by desire in this way is like a man dying of thirst who drinks a bowl of seawater: the more he drinks, the more thirsty he becomes.

244

There are limits to everything. If we want to be wealthy, maybe we will succeed in earning a tremendous amount of money, but one day circumstances will prevent us from gaining more and we will feel frustrated. Rather than coming up against limitations imposed from outside, it is better to fix our own boundaries. We should reduce our desires and learn to be content.

245

Desire is the source of endless problems. The more desires we have, the more we have to plan and work hard to realize them. Some time ago a businessman told me that the more he developed his company, the more he felt like making it even bigger. And the more he tried to make it bigger, the more he found he had to lie and fight mercilessly against his competitors. He had come to realize that wanting more and more made no sense, and that he only had to reduce the size of his business for competition to become less fierce so he would be able to carry out his work honestly. I found his testimony very true.

246

I do not mean to say that we should not do business or develop. Economic success is a good thing. In particular, it enables us to offer work to those who need it: business is good for oneself, for others and for society at large. If everyone lived a monastic life and begged, the economy would collapse and we would all die of starvation! [Laughs] I am convinced that what Buddha would do in such a situation would be to say to his monks: 'So now, all go out to work!' [Laughs]

247

The economy should not prosper at the expense of human values. We should stick to honest practice and not sacrifice our inner peace for profits. If everything were to be justified by profit, why did we abolish slavery? I believe that noble ideals are the true indices of progress.

Meditations on Jealousy

248

Jealousy makes us miserable and prevents us from progressing spiritually. If it is expressed as aggression, it also harms other people. It is a very negative emotion.

249

*J*ealousy is absurd. It does not stop those who make us jealous from having even more money or qualities, it only creates a new form of suffering in ourselves. And when it is strong enough to impel us to destroy the success or prosperity of others, what could be more base? There is no doubt at all that such actions will turn against us sooner or later.

250

Jealousy is absurd because a society's well-being is dependent on all the individuals that belong to it. If some prosper, society itself benefits and therefore, to some extent, we do too. When we see someone who is wealthy, rather than feeling irritated we should realize that their wealth also benefits us.

251

*I*f the person who makes us jealous is a dependent or someone we love, we can only rejoice in their success. If we do not have much respect for the person but their success is good for society, that is another reason to rejoice. We would be incapable of making our country prosperous by ourselves. It requires the concerted efforts and talent of many people. Since this person is one of these capable people, that is good news.

252

If those who are richer or more intelligent than us only use their success for their own benefit, what can we gain by suffocating ourselves through jealousy? Why shouldn't other people have the right to have what we ourselves wish we had?

253

There is a kind of jealousy which seems to me to be more justifiable, even though it is still a negative emotion. That is the jealousy felt in a couple when one partner's trust has been betrayed by the other. Suppose two people who really love each other decide to live together, get on well, trust each other completely, have children, and that one day one of them takes a lover or a mistress. One can easily understand that the other partner feels distressed.

The jealous party may share some responsibility for the situation, too. One person told me how he got married, but how, as he and his wife became more intimate and got to know each other better, he had felt more and more apprehensive and even averse to the idea that they would know everything about each other. Tension grew between them and his wife left to live with another man.

His reaction surprised me. When two people live together, it is quite normal that they should both become closer and closer. And the closer you are, the less you need to have secrets. Isn't it nice to be able to confide in someone completely? And isn't it ridiculous not to trust one's partner once one is married? If from the outset one has mistrust, then isn't it logical that the other person will look elsewhere for what he or she cannot find at home?

MEDITATIONS ON PRIDE

254

The worst defect of pride is that it prevents us from improving ourselves. If you think, 'I know it all, I am a truly good person', you won't learn anything and that is one of the worst things that can happen to you.

255

Pride also lies at the root of many social problems. It gives rise to jealousy, arrogance, contempt, indifference, and sometimes leads people to abuse and harm others.

256

*W*e must distinguish between pride and self-confidence. Self-confidence is necessary. It is what enables us, in certain situations, not to lose courage and to think with some justification, 'I am capable of succeeding'. Self-confidence is quite different from excessive self-assurance based on a false appreciation of our capacities or circumstances.

If you feel able to accomplish a task that other people cannot manage, then you cannot be called proud as long as your assessment is well founded. It is as if someone tall came across a group of short people who wanted to get something too high for them to reach, and said to them, 'Don't exert yourselves, I can do it'. This would simply mean that he was more qualified than the others to carry out a particular task, but not that he is superior to them or that he wants to crush them.

257

Pride is never justified. It is based on a mistaken evaluation of oneself, or on successes that are only temporary and superficial. We should remember its negative effects. We should also be aware of our defects and limitations, and realize that fundamentally we are no different from those we see as inferior.

Meditations on Trauma and Suffering

258

Some people have lived through dramatic events. They have witnessed their parents or others being massacred, they have been raped or tortured. Some years later, they are still haunted by those images and often find they cannot talk about them. Helping them is not straightforward. The seriousness of the trauma and the time it takes to heal depend in large measure on the social and cultural context. Religion can also play an important role. I think of Tibetans who, on account of their practice of Buddhism, are less vulnerable to tragic experiences.

259

*I*f the victims are sufficiently open-minded to forgive, and if those who have raped, tortured and killed recognize the enormity of their actions and wish to repent, then a meeting of both parties can be helpful. It can allow the perpetrator to acknowledge his mistakes and to express his sincere regret, and offers the victim a chance to unburden himself, at least partially, of his resentment. If both parties can find a ground for reconciliation, is this not the best way to proceed?

260

The victims themselves are not the only ones to be affected by serious conflict. Sometimes those who have inflicted suffering are troubled by it, too. I am thinking of the veterans of the Vietnam war who relive over and over again the violence and atrocity they committed. Even many years later they suffer from nightmares in which they revisit scenes with massacres, explosions, headless corpses and so on, and their minds are deeply disturbed.

261

*O*ften, the main problem faced by vulnerable people is the lack of emotional support offered by those around them. Kindness, altruism and compassion could help to relieve their suffering, but they are frequently lacking in our societies and the victims feel isolated and alone.

Nevertheless, it is possible to help them, to talk with them individually or in groups, and to apply different methods to relieve their torment. We should help them to realize that they are not alone, that many other people are in the same situation and many of those do succeed in overcoming it. Maybe we can talk to them about the suffering or traumas that we ourselves have been through, and explain how we managed to overcome them.

262

We cannot, of course, content ourselves with psychological theories and recipes. It is important to have pure intentions and to express oneself from the heart. One needs to be patient and prepared to persevere for as long as it takes. When a person's mind is deeply disturbed, it is not enough simply to mutter a few words of comfort.

263

Experience shows that those who have grown up in a peaceful atmosphere and who have been able to develop their human qualities in a stable way, react much better to trauma. Conversely, those who have come from backgrounds of conflict and violence usually react in a negative way and take longer to recover.

264

*I*n the same way as a strong body helps us to resist sickness and recover more quickly, a healthy mind enables us to bear tragic events or bad news more easily. If our mind is weak such events trouble us much more and for longer.

That does not mean that we are irredeemably conditioned from birth. Through training, one can always acquire better mental health. But here again education, the family environment, society, religion, the media, and many other factors all play a determining role.

265

*I*f you have lived through a tragedy, you should be aware that worry and anxiety are just an unnecessary addition to your suffering. Try to talk about your problem, release it and do not keep it secret on account of modesty or shame. Tell yourself that the problem is now over and there is no point in taking it with you into the future. Try to turn your mind to the most positive aspects of your life.

266

Reflect on the way your suffering came about. Those who harm others are slaves to the three mental poisons of ignorance, hatred, and desire, and cannot control their minds. Each one of us has these three poisons in us. They would only have to dominate us a little more and we, too, might commit extreme actions. Conversely, it is conceivable that a criminal could one day learn to control his or her negative emotions and become a kind person. One can never pass final judgement on anyone.

267

*O*n occasion, influenced by our tendencies or circumstances, we can do things that are normally unthinkable. Deluded by empty concepts such as racism or nationalism, people who are not criminals on the face of it commit acts of extreme violence and cruelty. We should remember this when we are harmed by others. And then we will be obliged to conclude that our suffering is the result of a great number of factors, and that it is impossible to lay blame entirely on one individual or on a single cause. We will then see the problem with different eyes.

Meditations on Shyness

268

Sometimes when we meet a stranger we can be excessively reserved and distant. This reaction is not logical. Actually, we have no good reason to fear contact with other people. We only have to realize that they are human beings like ourselves, with the same aspirations and the same needs, and it becomes easy to break the ice and communicate.

269

When I meet someone for the first time, I tell myself that above all the person is a human being who wishes to be happy and not to suffer, just like me. Age, size, skin colour, and social rank do not really matter; there is no fundamental difference between us. In this way, I can open up to that person as though he or she were a member of my own family, and all shyness disappears.

270

Shyness often stems from a lack of self-confidence and from too much attachment to formalities and social conventions. We are prisoners of the self-image we wish to present to others. Our behaviour then becomes artificial and our natural tendencies can sometimes remind us of this quite forcefully. When we have an urgent need to empty our bladder, we can pretend for a while that all is well but we cannot let the situation go on too long!

271

Shyness can also be a means of self-protection and an indication that we are too self-conscious. But, paradoxically, the more we protect ourselves the less self-confident we are and the more shy we become. On the other hand, the more we open to others and show love and compassion, the less we are obsessed with ourselves and the more confident we become.

Meditation on Indecisiveness

272

We need a minimum of courage in life in order to make decisions. But since it is not good to decide things impulsively, a certain dose of indecision is also necessary, just enough to evaluate the situation correctly or to take advice from those who are better informed. So indecision is useful to an extent. But once we have weighed the pros and cons, we need the strength to make our decision whatever problems we will have to face.

I have to admit that I do not always follow my own advice on this point. In meetings with the Kashag (the ministerial cabinet of the Tibetan government in exile), I have occasionally taken a decision on a topical issue and then, after lunch, another thought has occurred to me. Then I tell myself, 'I should have made a different decision!' [Peals of laughter] So in this regard, I do not have much advice to offer!

Meditations on Not Loving Yourself

273

Self-hatred is a very negative attitude. If we look deeply behind appearances, we realize that such hatred results from having too elevated an idea of who we are. We want to be the best at all costs, and if the slightest detail is missing from our ideal self-image we cannot bear it. This is a form of pride.

274

The first time I heard about self-hatred I was very surprised. I wondered how it was possible to hate oneself. All beings love themselves, even animals. Having reflected on this, I think it is just an exaggerated form of self-esteem.

275

*O*ne thing is certain. If we are not kind to ourselves, we cannot be kind to others. In order to love others and be tender, in order to wish them happiness and freedom from suffering, we must first have these feelings for ourselves. Then we will be able to understand that other people have the same aspirations as we do, and love and compassion become possible. If we hate ourselves, we cannot love others. And if we do nothing to change this attitude, we have little chance of finding inner peace and joy. We will waste our life and that is stupid. Perhaps I should not say these things but this is the truth.

276

*I*n order to transform self-hatred, we need to become aware that we have developed a false self-image and instead cultivate an authentic and healthy self-confidence based on our fundamental human qualities. We should be humble and more open to others.

MEDITATIONS ON ADDICTION TO ALCOHOL OR DRUGS

277

Those who are addicted to alcohol or drugs usually know that they are destroying themselves but cannot find in themselves the determination needed to stop. That weakness, just like vulnerability to trauma, is often a personality trait.

278

Everybody knows that drugs are harmful to health and confuse the mind. Even if they calm fear and anguish temporarily, they are incapable of extinguishing suffering altogether. They only mask it for a while. In order to overcome suffering, we must begin by understanding it and recognizing its nature and what causes it, and substance abuse makes such reflection impossible.

279

*I*n a BBC documentary, I heard young Russians say that the pleasure they derived from drugs far outweighed sexual pleasure, and yet that is supposed to be the most intense form of pleasure both for humans and animals. One can see how powerful these substances are in making us ignore the dangers to which they expose us. How could ignorance and confusion possibly deliver us from our problems? I often jokingly say that our mind is already sufficiently prey to distraction for extra distractions to be unnecessary.

280

Education, personal support and clear analysis of the negative effects of drugs can all help you to find the strength needed to drop them. Instead of looking for an immediate happiness that is artificial and fleeting and that inevitably ends in suffering, cultivate inner peace and happiness that are not dependent on circumstance or external support. Have confidence in your own nature and learn to stand on your own two feet. Open up more to other people. I am convinced that courage grows with altruism.

MEDITATIONS ON SEXUAL DESIRE

281

Generally, the way we label other people and things as good or bad, handsome or ugly, is determined by desire and craving. We call good what we like and bad what we dislike. These are inventions of our own minds. If beauty actually existed in objects themselves, we would all be irresistibly attracted by the same people and things.

282

Sexual desire, which channels all our senses together, is particularly powerful and can radically alter the way we see things. In sexual passion, the man or woman we desire appears perfect in every respect, unchanging and worthy of being loved for ever. Every detail of their being has an extraordinary aura to it. We cannot imagine living without them. But unfortunately, as everything changes by nature, what we perceive as adorable today can suddenly lose its attraction as a result of a few words or a gesture, however trivial. Worse still, if we discover that this person who we had thought was perfect loves someone else, they can all of a sudden appear quite reprehensible.

283

If sexual attachment weighs heavily on you, try to examine the situation in a relaxed way and from all possible angles. Consider that everything is continually changing and that goodness and beauty are only mental fabrications. Then your perspective will change. Sometimes, it is enough to ask yourself how you would perceive the object of your love if you suddenly learned that he or she was betraying you, or again, to imagine the person doing something that is incompatible with the ideal image you have of them.

284

We should distinguish clearly between true love and sexual attachment. The former, ideally, expects nothing in return and does not depend on circumstance. The latter can only change according to events and emotions.

285

Sexual relationships, which depend to a greater or lesser extent on sexual attraction, can only be genuine and lasting if the choice of partner is based not merely on physical attraction but on mutual understanding and respect.

MEDITATIONS ON SPEAKING MINDLESSLY

286

*I*t is often the case that we are mistaken in the way we see things and that we express this view through speech without intending to lie. There is a Tibetan story of a man who saw a big fish and who is asked how big the fish was. He replies, gesturing as he speaks, that the fish was really very large. People ask him to be more precise. How big exactly? Then the size of the fish becomes a little smaller. So, joking apart, how big really was it? This time, the fish has become really quite small. One cannot say that the man began by lying, he was simply not paying attention to what he was saying.

Strangely, certain people always seem to express themselves in this way. Tibetans are a case in point. When they tell a story, they do not offer any proof and nobody asks where the news came from or how the story came to pass. Those who tend to talk this way should pay more attention to what they are saying.

287

From one point of view it is a good thing to say little and to speak only when one has something to say. Language is one of the extraordinary characteristics of the human race, even though some animals such as dolphins and whales seem to have a complex form of communication. But if we look closely at human language, we realize how limited it is. Concepts and words isolate things artificially, whereas the objects they designate actually have innumerable facets that are constantly changing and that result from a set of equally innumerable causes and conditions.

As soon as we name an aspect of reality, we mentally eliminate all other aspects and we designate the chosen object by a word that applies only to that object and this enables us to recognize it. Then, according to how that object is used, we establish distinctions: this is good, that is bad and so forth, when in fact it is impossible to attribute intrinsic properties to anything. The result is a vision of reality which is at best partial and at worst plainly wrong. However rich language may be, its power is therefore very limited. Only non-conceptual experience enables us to apprehend the true nature of things.

288

The problem of language is found in many other fields as well – in politics, for example. Politicians develop simple policies to deal with complex problems that are linked to many different factors. They act as if they could find solutions by means of concepts and words, such as Marxism, Socialism, liberalism, protectionism, and so on. Amongst the host of causes and conditions responsible for any given situation, they isolate one or two and fail to take the others into account. They therefore never find an adequate response and misunderstandings are eminently possible. In my view, this itself is the source of many problems. Unfortunately, we have no option but to use words and concepts.

289

*I*t is best to use language only when it is useful to do so. To talk a lot unnecessarily is like allowing thousands of weeds to grow in a garden. Is it not better to have fewer?

Meditations on Criticizing Others

290

If someone criticizes me or even insults me, I willingly invite them to do so provided their intention is good. If we can see that someone has a fault and just say that there is nothing wrong, then that is pointless and does not help at all. If we tell the person that what they are doing is not too serious and later speak badly of them behind their back, that is not good either. We should say what we think to their face. We should clarify what is necessary, and separate truth from falsehood. If we have doubts then we should express them. Even if our words are a little harsh, we should say them anyway. It will clarify our thinking and any gossip will be unfounded. But if we confine ourselves to smooth-tongued and polite remarks, there will always be a basis for distorting rumour. Personally, I prefer direct talking.

291

*O*ne day someone said to me, 'According to Mao Zedong, one should have the courage to think, to speak and to act'. It is true that in order to work and carry out tasks we need to think. We also need the courage to say what we think and to do what we say. If people do not act, no progress is possible and no mistakes could ever be corrected. But we also need to ask ourselves whether what we are about to say and do will be useful.

292

If, with the best intention in the world, we say hurtful things to someone that do not actually help them, our aggressive and direct manner will not have achieved its goal. Maybe what the person needed was a white lie!

293

*I*n Hinayana Buddhism, the seven harmful actions of body and speech – killing, stealing, sexual misconduct, lying, slander, harsh words, and gossip – are forbidden. In Mahayana Buddhism, on the other hand, even an action as negative as killing is allowed if it is absolutely necessary for the benefit of others and is not associated with any selfish desire.

294

I think that in general we should tell the truth, and even if we express it harshly it can be beneficial. But we should avoid criticizing or insulting people, with a negative intention or a negative view of things. If we do that, our words will cause others to suffer, we will not feel good in ourselves and will only render the atmosphere oppressive and stifling.

MEDITATIONS ON CAUSING SUFFERING TO OTHERS

295

Sometimes we cause others to suffer out of ignorance, without even realizing that they are suffering. We are rarely conscious, for example, that animals also feel pleasure and pain. Nor do we really understand the suffering of our close relatives unless we have been through similar experiences ourselves. Of course, they are the ones who are suffering, not us. It is only by saying to ourselves, 'When someone beats me or insults me, I suffer in this way or in that way' that one may have an idea of what they are going through.

296

There are people who are not at all concerned about the harm they inflict on others. They believe the main thing is that they themselves come out of the situation unscathed. Once again, this problem stems from a lack of awareness. The more we make others suffer, the more we accumulate causes for our own future suffering. Furthermore, since we thereby harm society we are doubly harming ourselves.

297

If we have behaved very badly with someone we should feel regret. We should recognize our mistakes but without thinking that we can therefore no longer lead a normal life. We should not forget what we have done, but neither should we be crushed by depression or remorse. Neither should we be indifferent, which would be equivalent to ignoring what we had done, but instead we should learn to forgive ourselves: 'I have made mistakes in the past, but it will not happen again. I am a human being, so I am capable of freeing myself from my mistakes'. If we lose hope that means we have not forgiven ourselves.

298

*I*f possible we should go and see the person whom we have harmed, and tell them sincerely, 'I was unpleasant to you, I have made you suffer a great deal, please forgive me'. If the other person appreciates our repentance and their resentment dissolves, is this not what Buddhists call a 'restorative confession'?

299

*I*f you are not religious, it is enough to hold one's hand out to the person one has harmed, to acknowledge one's errors, to express one's sincere regret, and to pacify any grudges. Of course, for this to be possible both sides must be capable of considerable open-mindedness.

300

I do not think that the desire to harm is innate. It is not in us from birth, it comes later. It is one of our mental fabrications. Hitler began to think that Jews were harmful people who had to be eliminated, and this idea developed to the point that it eclipsed all others and chased away all feelings of compassion.

301

Seeing someone else as an enemy always stems from the imagination. And in Buddhist terms, it is considered artificial and fabricated in contrast to what exists naturally. A thought arises, one thinks it is true, one gives it great importance, one builds a plan on that basis and one implements the plan without considering the suffering that one is thereby inflicting on other people.

302

*I*n order to bring about a change of heart in those who act harmfully, we must begin by appealing to the depths of their humanity and try to find a way of detaching them as much as possible from their ideology. Only then is it possible to reason with them. If one does not manage to do this, all that remains is force. But not any type of force: even if other people have committed the most horrific crimes, we should always treat them humanely. This is the only viable method if we want them to change one day.

303

Love is the ultimate way to transform people, even when they are full of anger and hatred. If you express love continually and steadily, without ever tiring, you will touch them. This takes a lot of time. One needs tremendous patience. But if your intentions are perfectly pure and if your love and compassion are steady, you will succeed.

Meditations on Indifference

304

*I*ndifference, especially indifference towards other people, is one of the worst defects we can have. To think only of oneself, without caring about what is happening to one's neighbour, reflects a very narrow view of the world, a blinkered mind and a tightness of heart.

305

We depend on others from the moment we are conceived. The happiness and the future of our world, all the facilities we have, the simplest object that we use, our very survival from day to day, all result from the efforts of many people. Prayer and other spiritual practices also have a definitive effect, but it is mainly human activity that shapes the world.

306

Everything exists in relation to other things, in a state of interdependence. There is nothing that exists in and of itself. It is therefore impossible to conceive of one's own personal interests independently of those of others.

307

What we do in every moment brings about new circumstances, which themselves will contribute to the arising of other events. Whatever we do, we are participating, whether voluntarily or not, in the chain of cause and effect. In the same way, our future pleasure and suffering will result from present causes and conditions, even if the complexity of these connections escapes us. We are therefore responsible for ourselves and for others.

308

Anyone who is indifferent to the well-being of other people and to the causes of their future happiness, can only be laying the ground for their own misfortune.

MEDITATIONS ON RELIGIOUS BELIEF

309

Each one of us is free to believe or not believe. But once you follow a religion and believe in what it teaches, you should give it great importance in your life and avoid having faith only every other day. Do not act erratically and make sure that your thinking corresponds to what you say.

310

Some people think, 'If I believe in Buddhism, I must be able to live it completely and perfectly, otherwise I will drop it'. This attitude of all or nothing is common amongst Westerners. Unfortunately, it is difficult to reach perfection in a day.

311

*I*t is through gradual training that one reaches the goal: is this not an essential point? And you should not say to yourself, 'Whether I practise or not makes no difference, I will never get there'. Set a target, set in motion the means to reach it, and step by step you will get there.

312

Each one of us has our own nature and aspirations, and what suits one does not necessarily suit another. It is essential to bear this point in mind when we judge other religions and spiritual paths. The variety of religions matches that of people themselves, and even if religions do not see themselves in this way, it remains true that many people have found and continue to find religion a great source of support. We should keep this in mind and treat every religion with the respect it deserves. This is very important.

313

Each religion has its own rituals. But religions also have other aspects that are more fundamental. The essential practice of Buddhism, for example, is control of the mind. Even though it is not easy and requires assiduous effort, many of us consider this is of only secondary importance. In one way we believe in Buddhism, but in another we are incapable of going all the way with our belief. We are content with physical rituals, with superficial expressions of devotion and with texts that we recite only half-heartedly.

In Tibetan rituals we like to use drums, bells, cymbals, and other musical instruments. Onlookers think to themselves, 'These people are practising Buddhism!' But, in fact, we give a low priority to those contemplations that lead our mind to the world of delusion, or from love, compassion, and the enlightened mind, all of which are deeper practices to which we should be devoting all our energy. Is this not the case?

In Christianity, people go to Mass on Sundays and hurriedly recite a few prayers with their eyes closed, but when they have to face the problems of everyday life they have all sorts of ideas that are incompatible with their religion, and they are incapable of applying their faith or having the attitudes which Christ has taught.

In all these cases this means that we have not transformed ourselves, we are just like non-believers. We believe in religion during the ceremony, but we do not achieve the true goal of our faith.

314

Religion is rather like medical treatment. Medicines are effective when we are sick, not when we are in good health. When everything is fine, we do not show them to others saying, 'This remedy is excellent, this one is expensive, this is a nice colour'. Whatever they look like, their only function is to cure sickness. If they have no use at the moment, there is no reason to show them off.

In the same way, religions and spiritual paths must be useful and effective when our mind is in difficulty. If we show off our religion when everything is fine, and we are the same as other mortals in moments of crisis, then what is the point?

315

The crucial thing with religious beliefs is for our mind to merge with the teaching or practice that one receives, and to apply these in daily life. This is not something one can manage just like that. It comes gradually through training.

MEDITATIONS ON FOLLOWING NO RELIGION

316

There are many people who do not follow any religion. This is their right and nobody can force them to change. The important thing is that their life should be meaningful, in other words that deep down they should be happy. Happy, but without harming others. If our satisfaction means that others have to suffer, then sooner or later we will suffer too.

317

Life lasts at the most about a hundred years. This is very short compared with geological periods. If we spend this short time doing harm our life will have been pointless. Everyone has the right to happiness but nobody has the right to destroy the happiness of others. In no event can the goal of human existence entail making anyone suffer.

318

Even if we reach the height of knowledge or wealth, if we lack respect or compassion for other people our life is not worthy of a human being. To live happily while causing the least possible harm to others: this is the life to which all human beings have a right, and a life that is really worthwhile.

319

For the vast majority of us, happiness depends on material possessions. And yet it is obvious that possessions by themselves cannot bring us satisfaction. We only have to look around us. We can see people who have every conceivable comfort but who take tranquillizers or fall prey to alcoholism to find solace. Conversely, we can see people who have nothing but who are happy, relaxed, in good health, and who live to a great old age.

320

The most important thing is not the gross and immediate satisfaction of the senses but that of the mind. That is why to be good, to help others, to moderate one's desires and to be content with one's lot are not only the concern of people who follow a religion. I am not talking of these things as a means of pleasing God or ensuring a good rebirth. What I am saying is that anyone who would like to experience inner peace cannot do without them.

321

As economic and technological progress advances, we depend more and more closely on each other. Everything we do has an effect on the rest of the world, sooner or later. And, in its turn, the state of the world has repercussions on the happiness or misfortune of each individual. We can no longer get away with a narrow-minded vision as in the past, and take only one element into account, a single cause, or a single factor. Nowadays, each situation must be considered with all its facets.

322

I do not wish to imply that we must renounce our own happiness and dedicate ourselves exclusively to that of others. What I am saying is that the two are inseparable. If we are concerned about peace and happiness on Earth, we must learn to see things in a broad perspective and appreciate the importance of each person's actions.

323

There are about six billion human beings on this Earth. Amongst these, the majority are primarily interested in material comforts and hardly at all in religion or spirituality. Non-believers therefore make up the vast majority of humanity, and their way of thinking and behaving inevitably plays a crucial role in the evolution of the world. Luckily, it is not necessary to have a religion in order to act in a humane way; it is sufficient to be a human being!

324

Even animals who behave sociably attract other animals around them, while those which are violent cause them to run away. One often sees that aggressive dogs are given a wide berth by other dogs, even by those who are larger than them.

This applies all the more to humans. People who are in control of themselves, who have kind thoughts and pleasant speech, naturally have many friends. Other people feel good in their company and even animals like them. Wherever they go, they create such a pleasant atmosphere that people do not want to leave.

325

When our thoughts run wild, our speech is aggressive and our actions violent, other people will avoid us and feel uncomfortable as soon as they catch sight of us. They are not interested in what we have to say and turn away when we try to talk to them. How can they enjoy themselves or feel happy in our company? This makes life difficult, doesn't it?

326

Even though there are so many of us on this planet, everyone can only see themselves. We depend on others to eat, to have clothes, to find a job or become famous, and yet we regard other people as our enemies even though we are all so intimately connected. Is this not a patent contradiction?

327

We only have to show concern for others, in thought and act, for this life – not to mention future lives – to be a happy one, and for us to feel comfortable with ourselves; for there to be someone to support us whenever we have problems; and even for our enemies to become friends.

If we care only for ourselves and consider other people as enemies, we will be up against absurd difficulties of our own making. And if in this modern world life seems to be impossible without competition, we should remember that it is possible to do better than others without crushing them in the process.

MEDITATIONS ON MONASTICISM AND PRIESTHOOD

328

Most monastics give up family life. Celibacy is considered important in many religions for different reasons. In Buddhism, in order to reach enlightenment one must first free oneself from the mental poisons, starting with the most coarse. Now, the chief of these poisons, the one that binds us most assuredly to samsara and the cycle of rebirths, is craving or desire. If one studies the twelve interdependent links that depict the various stages of our enslavement to samsara, one realizes that without desire and its expression, the karma we have accumulated in the past could never take effect.

329

Amongst the various forms of desire, sexual desire is the most powerful because it implies attachment to the objects of the five senses simultaneously: form, sound, scent, taste and touch. That is why when we want to counteract desire, we begin by addressing its most burning expression. By reducing desire and cultivating contentment, we advance on the path of non-attachment. This is the Buddhist point of view. The other religious traditions each have their own way of explaining the process.

330

*O*n the practical level, monastic vows, including that of celibacy, free those who take them from some of the fetters that bind them. Nuns and monks who can detach themselves from mundane life do not have to worry about what others think of them. They dress cheaply and their material needs are reduced to a minimum.

331

When you are married, whether you like it or not, you are prisoner to a certain number of social constraints. Expenditure is much higher than when you live alone, and the more we spend, the more we have to work, make calculations and make plans. The more we work and make plans the more difficulties we face, and the more we are tempted to undertake actions that will harm others. There are tremendous advantages when we move from family life to the life of a renunciant – like, for example, the life of Christian nuns and monks who pray, read and meditate five or six times a day, and who have hardly any worldly activities or goals.

332

At the moment of death, the renunciant is more serene. Others often have many other worries. 'What will my child do? How will he go to school? What will he live on? And what will become of my wife? How will my elderly husband survive without me? My young wife will probably end up living with another man.' Aren't troubles such as these exactly what we can do without at the moment of death?

In many countries, the father is the family's only breadwinner. If he dies, his widow finds herself destitute and often wonders how she is going to survive. If she has children, her situation is even more critical.

333

Before we marry, we are anxious because we have not yet found a spouse. After we have married, we are no happier for it. The man wonders whether his wife is still listening to him, while the woman wonders whether her husband still finds her attractive. It's complicated.

334

Marriage itself is a very expensive affair. The celebrations have to be grand. In India, people spend a large part of their wealth on it. They save up, even to the point of rationing their meals. Once the ceremony is over, some couples suffer because they are unable to have children, while others do conceive but don't want children and have them aborted.

Is it not far simpler to avoid all such troubles? Monks and nuns occasionally think they might be better off being married, but if they can drop this thought isn't their life a more peaceful one? The life of a single person is really far more serene.

335

Certain people will think that my view on this is selfish. I am not so sure. People get married for their own benefit, not that of others. And they often fail to meet even this limited objective. As for those who take vows of celibacy, like Christian nuns and monks, they can devote themselves entirely to helping others and to caring for the sick. I am thinking of Mother Teresa who had no husband or children, no family ties, and who dedicated all her time to the poor. With a family this is much more difficult. Even when the will is there, there is the housework to do, the children to take to school, and all the rest.

336

*I*n our Tibetan government in exile, if we send a monk somewhere on a mission he can leave immediately. If we ask him to go abroad, no problem. If we ask him to come back, he does so immediately. If you ask the same thing of a businessman you will find it is much more complicated. He might say, 'I have just opened a new store, I have to stay here, I'm sorry …'

337

I wish to say a few words about monastics who teach. Tsongkhapa used to say that whatever spiritual path one follows, it is not appropriate to try to change others if one has not transformed oneself. If we teach the defects of anger, for example, we should not get angry ourselves, otherwise we find it hard to be convincing. The same applies to teaching about moderating our desire and cultivating contentment.

338

A lama whom I know once wrote to me saying that in Nepal, for the last thirty years, Tibetans have built many monasteries with sumptuous temples and expensive statues, but that over the same period they had not built a single school or a single hospital. I am sure that in their place Christian priests would not have done this. There are also young lamas who usually wear monastic robes, and who in the evening don a suit and attend worldly receptions where they behave like VIPs or rich businessmen. I wonder whether the Buddha would have acted in this way.

339

This is the painful truth: the Buddha preached humility and devotion to others, but we take no notice. In my view, this is a case of hypocrisy that would benefit from being denounced in the press. That is the only way.

The Buddha said that we must teach others according to their needs and live according to what we teach. We should therefore apply the precepts to ourselves before sharing them with others.

Meditation on Leading a Contemplative Life

340

Like other religions, Buddhism includes a number of teachings that are studied in a speculative way and transmitted from master to disciple, but it is the contemplatives who discover the full depth of the teachings by bringing them alive through personal experience. Although there are few of them, they truly carry what we call the 'victory banner' of spiritual practice. By means of mental calm and profound insight, they attain meditative experiences and inner realization, thereby breathing life into theoretical knowledge which otherwise tends to be rather mythical or artificial. I can only encourage them.

Meditations on Faith

341

There is no doubt that faith plays a very important role in every religion. But it must be motivated by valid reasons. Nagarjuna, the great Indian philosopher of the second century CE, said that knowledge and faith should go hand in hand. It is true that in Buddhism we consider faith as a source of high rebirths and knowledge as a source of enlightenment, but it is also said that 'faith springs from clear knowledge'; in other words, we must know why we believe.

342

Buddhists distinguish three stages or levels of faith: inspiration, desire and conviction. Inspired faith is the kind of admiration you might feel by reading a text, meeting an exceptional person or hearing someone speak about the Buddha. Faith based on desire involves the idea of emulation: we aspire to know, to go deeper and to become the same as what we admire. Both these kinds of faith are unstable because they are not founded on true understanding. Faith based on conviction, on the other hand, is based on a clear understanding that what we aspire to is possible. It is supported by reasoning. In the Sutras, the Buddha asks his disciples not to believe blindly in what he tells them, but to test his words just as a goldsmith tests the purity of gold by beating it, heating it and pulling it.

343

*U*nless devotion is solidly established there is a risk that it will be only temporary. Some Buddhists – Tibetans and others – have tremendous devotion for a spiritual master. But as soon as that master dies they suddenly lose it. They think that it's all over, and their local Buddhist centre closes. And yet, ultimately, whether the master is present in flesh and bone makes no difference. The master represents the ultimate nature of the mind, and the compassion of him or her is not limited by distance. Anyone who recognizes the true dimension of the master will not tend to be attached to his human form. He knows that even though the master has left his or her physical casing, in the sphere of the absolute his blessings and activity continue.

344

If we feel that once our master has left this world our devotion no longer has a focus, that means it was mixed with attachment. We were attached to our master as to a companion, an ordinary being, a partner, a loved one. In such a case, when the master dies he completely disappears and we are lost. What we felt for him was undoubtedly not true devotion.

Meditations on Sectarian Prejudice

345

I can see two possible ways of being non-sectarian in religious matters. On the one hand, we can have respect for all religions. For example, I am a Buddhist, but at the same time I have great respect for Christianity and the other religions. On the other hand, we might feel respect for other religions and also wish to practise them. Thus we see some people who practise Christianity and Buddhism at the same time. This is perfectly possible, to a point.

346

When we become more engaged along the path, things become more complicated. When we deepen our understanding of 'emptiness' and the interdependence of all things[3], it is difficult to accept at the same time the idea of a Creator God who exists in and of Himself and who is unchanging. Similarly, for someone who believes in a God who created the universe interdependence poses a problem. On a certain level one begins to touch upon the very foundation of one's religion and then one is obliged, so to speak, to specialize. This does not preclude at all the possibility of respecting all paths, it simply makes it difficult to follow them all at once.[4]

3. 'Emptiness', as it is understood in Buddhism, does not mean nothingness, rather it refers to the simple fact that nothing by itself has intrinsic reality.

4. The Dalai Lama sometimes says that the notion of God is not problematic for Buddhists as long as God is thought of as infinite love. It is a problem if God is seen as a first cause.

347

*I*n Buddhism there is a practice called 'taking refuge'. When we take refuge in the Buddha, I am not sure that we can also take refuge in Christ, for example, without facing a dilemma. I think it is preferable in such a case to consider Christ as the emanation of a bodhisattva.

Meditations on Becoming a Buddhist

348

As a general rule, I think the religion our parents follow is the most appropriate for us to follow too. In addition, it is not good to follow a religion and then to change to another one.

349

These days many people are interested in spirituality, and especially in Buddhism, but they do not check carefully enough to see what they are committing to. You must first be certain that the path you choose is appropriate for your nature and your aspirations. Ask yourself whether you are capable of practising it, and what benefit it might bring you. Study its basic teachings. You will not be able to understand everything about Buddhism before you have committed to practising it, but you can acquire a sound knowledge of its essential points. You should then reflect seriously on these. If after careful examination you decide to follow it, that is fine. Only then should you commit yourself further and if necessary take vows.

350

There are many forms of meditation in Buddhism. They can be analytical, or focused on a single object, or non-conceptual, or profound absorptions; they can focus on impermanence, the lack of ego, suffering, love, compassion, and so on. But in order to practise these correctly, it is necessary to follow the instructions of an experienced and trustworthy master.

The master who teaches you Buddhism therefore has a major role. That is why you should also learn about the qualities that make a true master, check to see whether your master has them and decide whether you are determined to follow him or not.

351

Act cautiously. Above all, avoid becoming a Buddhist without reflecting on it first, without knowing anything about the religion but simply acting on a whim, only to find later on that this or that practice does not suit you or seems impossible.

352

When some people hear that a lama is teaching somewhere, they rush to hear him and trust him without knowing anything about him, and without taking time to see whether or not he has the necessary qualities. After a while, they discover that he has certain weaknesses.

They hear that a lama is staying nearby and commit themselves to him immediately, without really knowing him. They receive teachings, particularly initiations, and one day their attitude changes diametrically to the opposite. They explode in anger, shouting out to whoever will listen that the lama has sexually abused their girlfriend, and while they are at it they rail against Buddhism as a whole. Such people only discredit the true teachings, and when they commit themselves to unqualified lamas they claim that the Buddha is responsible for their heartbreak. What is the meaning of this? Their attitude is not right. Before committing themselves they should have been better informed.

353

The preliminary examination of a master is a very important step that is often mentioned in Buddhist texts. If one establishes a spiritual connection with a master in an unconsidered way, once the defects of this ill-chosen person come to the surface, one obviously experiences it as a disaster. Nevertheless, once we have received vows and initiations, it is best not to give free rein to negative thoughts.

354

Everyone, whoever it is, has both qualities and defects. The texts say that a spiritual master should have more qualities than us, but what does that actually mean? Let's suppose that someone has received from a master the rare oral transmission of a particular teaching. Even if the master does not have much knowledge, purely from the point of view of that transmission he or she does have something we do not have, and in that sense he is superior to us.

355

If we are connected spiritually to an inauthentic master and have received Buddhist teachings from him, he is nevertheless worthy of our appreciation. From this point of view, it is inappropriate to see him as an ordinary person or, worse still, to suddenly detest him. Even if we regret the relationship he has become our spiritual guide and it is better to avoid such extreme reactions.

This does not mean that we have to continue to receive his instructions. We are free not to see him again. When you have received Buddhist teachings from someone, the best thing, if you can, is to cultivate faith in him. If this is not possible then remain neutral without entertaining either good thoughts or bad.

356

When you practise Buddhism, do not expect to be able to fly through the sky, penetrate material objects or see the future. The main goal of the practice is to tame one's own mind, not to acquire miraculous powers. It so happens that when we do tame our mind we can, as a side-effect, gradually acquire powers that are said to be miraculous. But if we make these our main goal, I seriously doubt whether what we are practising can be called Buddhism. Non-Buddhists also acquire such powers. Apparently even the KGB and CIA were interested in them a few years ago. So be careful.

Meditations on Practising Buddhism

357

When one begins to follow a spiritual path one is full of courage, then one starts expecting results and finally one gets tired and blasé. That is the sign that our view is too short-sighted. It is a mistake to expect quick results, unless we make the sort of effort made by the yogi Milarepa. Is it not significant that, according to the scriptures, the Buddha required three incalculable aeons[5] to reach complete enlightenment? How can we possibly imagine that we can get there after just a few years in retreat? That simply shows that we are not familiar with the teachings. To imagine, as we sometimes do, that by shaking a bell[6] for three years we can attain buddhahood is just not serious.

5. An extremely long period of time; 'incalculable' here refers to the highest number used in ancient Indian arithmetic.

6. The bell, which symbolizes emptiness or wisdom, one of the most profound principles of Buddhism, is commonly used in Tantric Buddhist rituals. Here, the Dalai Lama is speaking sarcastically. He is denouncing those who are content with ritual and who make no effort to grasp the essence of the teachings.

358

*I*t is wonderful to be enthusiastic about Buddhist practice, but when we say that the Buddha accumulated merit and wisdom through three incalculable aeons, we should consider that that is the time that is needed in order to reach final enlightenment. According to Mahayana, the Buddha had attained enlightenment long ago in the wisdom body. He then appeared in the manifestation body and pretended to go through the process of enlightenment all over again from the beginning. But then, did he not have good reason to act in this way? We who are learning to follow in his footsteps, should never forget to reflect on the fact that even in his last life he spent another six years practising austerities. Maybe this will help us not to have a short-sighted view.

359

*I*t is true that by means of the quick path of Vajrayana, it is said that one can attain buddhahood very rapidly, without abandoning negative emotions. But this is risky. In Milarepa's biography one lama tells him, 'Whoever meditates on my teaching during the daytime becomes a buddha during the daytime, whoever meditates on it at night becomes a buddha at night, and fortunate beings who have a favourable karma have no need to meditate on it at all.' Milarepa, convinced as he was that he must be one of those fortunate individuals, spent his time sleeping. If we misinterpret things like this, there is a risk we will be over-enthusiastic to begin with but grow tired very quickly. If, on the other hand, our enthusiasm is based on a true understanding of how the path works, it will not fail. It is essential to understand this.

360

Religions teach precepts or moral guidelines that help to emphasize human qualities. Some people, particularly in Buddhism, neglect this moral aspect and focus only on meditation from which they expect to derive miraculous results. When they realize that this is not happening they are naturally disappointed.

361

The goal of the practice is not to obtain miraculous powers but to transform our being. The main problem is that we are not ready to devote the necessary time to this. We know that the Buddha needed aeons, and yet we imagine that for us two or three years will suffice. That is why, in my view, the Mahayana path is indispensable. Once we have a good knowledge of this path, if we have a growing interest in Vajrayana we will then have enough determination to follow it, even if it takes three aeons. Armed with courage of this kind, we will be able to practise Vajrayana as a means of instilling mental calm and profound insight quite effortlessly, and we will have every chance of succeeding.

362

*I*f we rush into Vajrayana without establishing a solid foundation of practice, we might think that we can attain buddhahood easily 'in one lifetime and in one body', as it is said in the scriptures. It is also possible to identify the imaginary deity on whom one meditates with the creator of the universe, and to think that if we have faith in that deity he or she will bestow powers upon us, a long life, prosperity and I don't know what else. At that point, we are no longer focused on the main objective which is freedom from the mental poisons, and we are attaching too much importance to secondary things.

363

Some people do not particularly have faith in the Buddha's teaching, but are interested in it from a purely academic point of view. Yet others have faith in the teaching but limit themselves to studying it intellectually and acquiring only theoretical knowledge of it. The problem is that the only aim of the teaching is to help us transform our being, not to help us acquire more information than we already have. If, having learned about it, we do not put it into practice through meditation, it will have been completely useless. Then we risk becoming a hardened Buddhist, someone who knows the Buddhist teaching in theory and who knows how to talk about it, but who has not tasted it because he or she has not transformed it into a living experience. By contrast, when we do apply the teaching to ourselves, we discover its true flavour and the risk of becoming hardened fades away. We must therefore merge the teaching closely with our own mind. Understanding and practice must go together.

364

Those who want to lead a contemplative life and undertake long retreats, such as the three-year retreat that was traditionally practised in Tibet, should prepare themselves well by means of the preliminaries.[7] To stay enclosed between four walls without having accomplished these practices, designed to turn our mind towards the spiritual path, is rather like serving a prison sentence. If during the meditation sessions one simply recites mantras without really thinking about anything in particular, the retreat is pointless. One will have started the retreat as an ordinary being and by the end nothing will have changed. On top of this, one might be prouder than before because one might tell oneself that since one has been enclosed for three years one deserves being called a 'lama'. What is the point?

7. The 'preliminaries' are practices that prepare the mind for receiving and applying the practices called 'the main practices'.

But by completing the preliminaries with care and engaging regularly in the main practices, and only after that doing a three-year retreat, one can be sure that by the end one will be able to think, speak and act differently. At the very least one will be disciplined, and that is a good start.

365

*I*f as a Buddhist you wish to dedicate yourself to humanitarian work, that is a good thing. Check that your intention is perfectly pure. But nevertheless, social action is not in itself an engaged form of Buddhism if it is not carried out with love and compassion, and if one does not take refuge in the Buddha.[8]

This is why you should devote part of your time to practice sessions, during which you take refuge and meditate on impermanence, suffering, and so forth.

8. Taking refuge is one of the basic practices for all Buddhists. It means taking the Buddha as one's guide, his teaching as one's path, and the community of practitioners as one's companions along the way. At a deeper level or at a later stage of the practice, it means recognizing one's own ultimate nature as the Buddha himself.